BOOKS ON SPORTS

For boys and girls, men and women, for all from the beginner to the top professional, for the leisure-time sportsman and for the serious competitor.

More than 100 titles are offered in the following sports:

BASEBALL • BASKETBALL • BOATING • BOWLING •
BOXING • CAMPING • CANOEING • CHEERLEADING •
FENCING • FIGURE SKATING • FISHING • FOOT-
BALL • GOLF • HANDBALL • HOCKEY • HORSEBACK
RIDING • HUNTING • LACROSSE • PHYSICAL CONDI-
TIONING • ROPING • SAILING • SELF DEFENSE •
SKIING • SOCCER • SOFTBALL • SWIMMING AND
DIVING • TENNIS • TRACK AND FIELD • TUMBLING •
VOLLEYBALL • WRESTLING

The RONALD SPORTS LIBRARY (incorporating the original Barnes Sports Library) is recognized as one of the most complete and widely used lists of sports books available anywhere in the world. The series consists of instructional, how-to books profusely illustrated and brief in length.

The OUTDOOR SPORTSMAN'S LIBRARY is another featured series. Hunters, fishermen, campers, and water sports enthusiasts will find good reading here.

Advanced books are available for the mature sports reader as well as a diversified list of textbooks and reference volumes in the area of physical education.

SURF
FISHING

Vlad Evanoff

ILLUSTRATED BY
THE AUTHOR

Second Edition

THE RONALD PRESS COMPANY • NEW YORK

2

Library of Congress Catalog Card Number: 58-7376

Preface

Of all the different kinds of salt-water fishing one of the most difficult forms is surf fishing. It requires more skill, experience, and knowledge than most of the other types. In fact, it takes a long time to become a skilled surf angler. Many beginners become discouraged when they find that it takes years to acquire the technique necessary to surf fishing.

About the nearest thing to a short cut is to have a veteran surf angler take you under his wing and let you accompany him on fishing trips. But there aren't too many such old-timers who are willing to do this. And first you have to find them and make their acquaintance.

You can also join one of the many surf fishing clubs found in our coastal states. Here you will meet other surf anglers who will teach you and invite you on fishing trips. You can also read magazines which publish articles on surf fishing to pick up some information. Such publications as the *Salt Water Sportsman* and the *Fisherman* Magazine often print surf fishing articles and tips on the sport.

However, it will still take a lot of time to acquire all the facts and skills needed for surf fishing. So any additional help you can obtain will prove useful. That is one of the purposes of this book—to cover surf fishing broadly and at the same time to bring out those small details which are often overlooked in most written material on the subject. If this work helps shorten the way for the beginner and offers some useful suggestions to the veteran angler, the author will be satisfied and more than repaid for his efforts.

The author owes a debt of gratitude to the following: Frank Woolner, editor of the *Salt Water Sportsman,* for supplying the illustrations of Massachusetts surf fishing; G. G. Smith, of the Enterprise Manufacturing Co., and Dick Wolff, of the Charles Garcia Corporation, for the use of their photographs; and to the Florida News Bureau, the Rhode Island Development Council, and the New Jersey Department of Conservation and Economic Development for photographs of surf fishing in their areas.

VLAD EVANOFF

Contents

Chapter 1

Conventional Tackle

The conventional or standard surf fishing outfit had its beginnings almost one hundred years ago. As far back as 1865 members of the Cuttyhunk Fishing Club on the island of Cuttyhunk, Massachusetts, were using salt-water rods and revolving spool reels for striped bass fishing. Of course, these early rods were shorter in length and were usually made from some solid wood, such as lancewood or greenheart. The reels were crude brass models which lacked such modern refinements as free spools, star drags, or anti-backlash devices. However, the basic principle of using these early outfits was similar to that of today's conventional surf fishing tackle.

Through the years the conventional surf fishing outfit has been perfected until today it still reigns supreme as the most versatile surf fishing tool. Other types of tackle may surpass or equal it under some conditions and for certain kinds of fishing, but for day in and day out use under varying conditions and for most surf fishing, you can't beat the conventional surf fishing outfit.

Surf rods can be divided into three classes: light, medium, and heavy. The light surf rod will run from about 8 to 9½ ft. in over-all length (butt and tip). If it comes in two sections, the tip section will be from 6 to 7½ ft. long and the butt will usually run from 20 to 28 in. This rod will have a fairly thin, limber tip, and can handle lures from 1 to 2½ oz. and sinkers up to 3 or 4 oz. Most practical for fishing in calm waters or light surf and where there are no obstructions around, it is also ideal for such smaller gamefish as bluefish and school stripers and for such bottom feeders as the whitings or kingfish, croakers, surf perch, and so on.

The medium weight surf rod—the "all-purpose" stick for surf fishing—runs from 9 to 10 ft. in over-all length. If it is a two-piece rod, the tip section will run from 6½ to 7½ ft. and the butt will be anywhere from 22 to 28 in. Such a rod will be limber but will have enough

1

The conventional surf outfit is still supreme when fishing for big fish, using heavy lures in strong currents. This 63-lb. striper was taken by Frank Machado in the Cape Cod Canal in Massachusetts.

backbone to handle big fish in fairly heavy currents, tides, or surf. The lures it casts are from 1 to 3½ oz. and the sinkers are up to 4 or 5 oz., which is the nearest thing to an "all-around" rod for surf fishing in most areas. Its lightness will provide fun and sport with the smaller species, yet the rod is strong enough to handle the biggest fish, too. Also, it can cast most of the lures used in surf fishing, besides doing a creditable job in bait fishing.

The heavy surf rod is the "big gun" of the surf. Alternately called a "production" stick, its length runs anywhere from 9 to 11 ft. In two sections the tip may be from 7 to 8½ ft. long while the butt may run from 26 to 32 in. Such a heavy duty rod is mostly a specialized outfit reserved for certain areas and conditions: Cape Cod, Montauk, parts of Rhode Island, North Carolina, or any other place where long casts and heavy lures or sinkers and baits may be used. Essen-

CONVENTIONAL SURF ROD

tially it is a big fish rod most practical in a heavy surf or strong current, but it also enables an angler to handle big fish in rocky areas where a fish must be turned or stopped because of nearby obstructions. However, a heavy surf outfit is more tiring when used for any length of time.

Not too long ago surf rods were being made from several kinds of materials, but today glass fiber is used mostly, although a few split-bamboo rods are still around. A good, hollow-glass surf rod is light, strong, and less affected than split-bamboo by heat, cold, or moisture. A glass rod is best for the average surf angler.

Surf rods come in one or two pieces. The one-piece rods have better action and are somewhat lighter since many are made up with a single glass blank and the other fittings around it. There is no heavy reel seat or wood butt to add weight. However, a one-piece rod occupies more space, must be transported outside the car on rod-carriers, and can't be tucked away neatly in a closet. Most surf anglers who don't live near the beach and must transport their rod inside the car or a bus or train prefer the two-piece one.

Which outfit—light, medium, or heavy—is best for you? That's something every angler will have to decide for himself. If you can afford it and do a lot of surf fishing, you'll find that eventually you'll want all three outfits. This will allow you to go to any part of the country and be prepared for all kinds of surf fishing. If you don't do too much fishing or can't afford to lay out the money for all three outfits, then the medium weight surf rod is best. This is also most suitable for the beginner since he has no idea of where he will do most of his fishing and what he will catch. If you already have a medium or heavy outfit, you can get a light outfit to use on small fish and for casting light lures. If you plan to fish in an area where long casts with heavy lures or sinkers will be made, then a heavy outfit will be more practical.

The length of the rod and butt depends on a person's build—his height and arm length. A short man will have trouble handling the very long rods, while a tall, husky bruiser will prefer them. Similarly a man with long arms will feel cramped with a short butt, and a man with short arms will have trouble with a long butt. Try out the various lengths to see which one fits you best. If possible, try casting with a friend's rod to get an idea. A good tackle dealer who knows his surf tackle and surf fishing can also recommend the proper rod for you.

The type of fishing you do, where you fish, and what you catch also govern the choice of surf rod. If you plan to fish mostly with natural bait, then you'll find the heavy or medium rod most practical. Here the rod tip and butt can be as long as you can handle since you don't make many casts and the extra weight and length is no handicap. But the longer, heavier surf rods make it easier to handle the heavier sinkers and baits and to cast the long terminal rigs and leaders.

If, on the other hand, you will do mostly "squidding" with artificial lures of varying weights, you should get the medium weight outfit. This is often called a squidding rod. If you will fish mostly from sand beaches or places where long casts are needed, this medium rod can be long. Fishing from rock jetties, breakwaters, or rocky shores with deep water nearby will require only a shorter rod. If most of the fish run small, and you are fishing open beaches with no obstructions around, the light outfit will provide the most sport and fun. There are a dozen or more manufacturers who make good surf rods.

After you have the rod the next item to consider is the reel. Conventional surf reels have been perfected through the years until they are almost foolproof. Today's product is a wonderful, precision mechanism that performs smoothly and lasts for years if taken care of properly. A surf reel receives a lot of punishment from salt water, sand, heat, cold, friction, and continuous wear and tear. Most of the reels made by such reputable companies as Penn, Ocean City, and Pflueger are good products.

A good surf reel has a wide light metal or plastic spool, which should be light to prevent overruns or backlashes. Although most so-called "squidding" reels have wide spools, I prefer slightly narrower ones in order to spool the line back on the reel more evenly (this is especially important when night fishing). But for any casting, for that matter,

SPOOL   FREE SPOOL LEVER

STAR DRAG

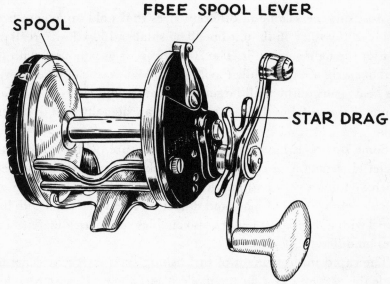

CONVENTIONAL SURF REEL

an evenly spooled line casts with less trouble. Some reels are made
with level-winding devices which put the line back on the reel evenly.
However, some of these reels cut down on your casting distance and
require more cleaning, oiling, and other care.

A surf reel should also have a free spool and a star drag. The star
drag, is, of course, standard today on surf reels and is necessary in
fighting big fish. The newer "starless" drag reels put out by Ocean
City are also used. These are really drag reels similar to the others
but they lack the "star" on the outside of the handle. Those with star
drags require turning of the star to adjust the drag, but the starless
type can be adjusted by merely cranking the handle forward or backing off. When you turn the handle forward, the drag increases; when
you back off the handle, it decreases. This is a big advantage when
playing a big, lively fish.

Surf reels have a gear ratio of at least 3 to 1 for retrieving the line
more rapidly. Many surf reels now have anti-backlash devices to prevent backlashes during a cast. Helpful to the beginner and very useful for night fishing, most of them can be adjusted to match the weight
of the lure being used. However, most expert surf anglers still rely on
their thumbs since anti-backlash devices tend to shorten the distance
of the cast.

Most surf reels come in different sizes that hold anywhere from 150 to 250 yds. of 36-lb. test line. The smaller 150-yd. size reels are best for the light surf outfit. The 200-yd. size is usually used with the medium weight outfit, while the larger 250-yd. reels can be used with the heavy surf outfit. Still larger reels are sometimes used for shark fishing in the surf, but they are heavy and are actually boat or trolling reels.

Some surf reels have a "take-apart" feature, which enables the angler to clean, oil, or change spools quickly. This is especially useful when you get a very bad tangle or lose a lot of line. Then you can quickly remove the old spool and substitute a new one filled with line. A reel with a take-apart feature also enables you to use different sized lines on different spools.

The rapid improvement of surf fishing lines in recent years has made things a lot easier for the modern surf angler. It wasn't too long ago that the surf angler using linen lines had to dry them carefully, examine them each fishing day, and contend with swelling which increased the diameter and cut down casting distance. Today linen lines have almost disappeared from the surf fishing scene, and have been replaced by nylon, dacron, and nylon-dacron combinations. The braided nylon lines have been used in surf fishing for many years now and are still popular because they are waterproof, thin in diameter, don't rot, and cast smoothly. Dacron has many of the same properties but, in addition, is even thinner in diameter than nylon and has less stretch. Some line companies are also combining nylon and dacron in the same line. Whichever line you choose is a matter of personal preference. They are all good and give you your money's worth compared with the old-time linen lines. They'll last for several years if you don't fish too often or around rocks or mussels. About the only complaint one has against the synthetic lines is that they fray and cut readily when dragged against abrasive surfaces like rocks.

The size of the line will depend on the fishing you plan to do, where you will fish, the weight of the fish, the lures used, and the outfit you have. With a light outfit lines testing 25 to 30 lbs. are best. For medium weight outfits the 36-lb. test line is used, which is the best all-around size for both artificial lures and bait fishing. When fishing in heavy currents, around rocks, and when seeking big fish, a 45-lb.

test line is safer. It is also good with the larger reels and heavier rods.

After a surf angler gets a rod, reel, and line, he is far from being properly equipped. There are many accessories which are required to make surf fishing more successful, safer, and comfortable. First on the list is a pair of hip boots or chest-high waders. If you fish mostly in warmer climes or from high rocks and jetties where you don't do much wading, a pair of rubber boots will often serve the purpose. These can be used in combination with a pair of waterproof overall pants, which are slipped over the boots to keep the waves and spray from getting inside. However, you still can't wade out into the water deeper than the boot tops.

The well-equipped surf angler wears a waterproof jacket with hood, waders, and a small bag or pouch for lures, but he still leaves his hands free for casting and playing a fish.

For all-around use a pair of chest-high, all rubber waders are best. They weigh quite a bit and are expensive, but they provide protection and warmth and enable you to wade out on a sand bar or into the surf farther than with boots. When you buy waders make sure they are on the loose side, since you may wear heavy pants and socks underneath. Try them on for size to see if you can raise your legs with ease. If not, get a different pair, since you'll have trouble walking and climbing rocks with binding waders.

Plastic waders can also be used for surf fishing along sandy beaches or in southern waters. Although light and less expensive, they don't stand up well enough around rocks, barnacles, or mussels to be used on rocky shores or jetties.

Next on the list is a waterproof jacket which can be worn over the waders. Such a parka designed especially for surf fishing has a hood, waterproof seams, and drawstrings or snaps around the neck, waist, and cuffs to keep the water and rain out.

For fishing jetties, breakwaters, or rocky shores where the going is slippery, a pair of ice-creepers or wading sandals is a must. It's bad enough keeping your balance on a small rock and casting even with such protection, but it is often dangerous without them. The ice-creepers or wading sandals are bought in most coastal fishing tackle stores. Many surf anglers make their own ice-creepers or wading sandals by using leather, metal, and rubber.

One of the handiest items a surf angler can own is a surplus pistol belt, which can be found in almost any army-navy war surplus store. This has reinforced holes scattered along its length for attaching various pouches, snaps, gaff, stringer, and similar items. The whole belt can be put on and taken off in a jiffy and is very convenient.

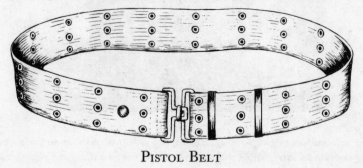

PISTOL BELT

The pouches for holding lures can also be bought in the same stores. However, if you use many wooden or plastic plugs in the large sizes, you'll find a regular plug container most suitable. These are sold in some coastal tackle stores, or they can be made from silverware trays and canvas bags. When such a container is attached to the pistol belt it is within easy reach and holds from six to eight large plugs. A separate small pouch can be attached to the belt to hold metal squids or jigs.

The beach fisherman who does a lot of bait fishing or spends a whole day surf fishing in a small area will find a large shoulder bag ideal. There are many such big bags for sale to hold sinkers, hooks, spare reel, pliers, leaders, and even a lunch or a thermos bottle.

The surf angler who often needs a gaff to land his fish finds this especially true when fishing from high rock jetties or breakwaters. Here a long-handled gaff anywhere from 6 to 8 ft. long is best. When fishing from beaches or wading out on a sand or rock bar, a short gaff which can be worn at the waist is the type to get. This should have some kind of protective cover over the point so that you don't get stuck.

A fish stringer is a much needed item in surf fishing, provided, of course, that you catch the fish to put on it. If you are wading and fishing far out from shore on a bar, you will find that it saves the time and trouble of bringing each fish up on shore. You put the fish on the stringer and let them swim around in the water behind you. But a stringer is also good for securing fish around a rock when on a jetty and for dragging a big fish or a mess of fish through the water along a sandy beach. Some surf anglers prefer chain for stringers while others use a heavy rope such as nylon anchor rope. A fish stringer should be at least 8 or 10 ft. long.

The headlight used by surf anglers fishing at night should have an elastic band which goes around the neck to hold the light high on the chest. The batteries are in a tight case worn under the parka on your pants belt. With such a light your hands are free for casting and fishing.

The beach fisherman using bait will find a sand spike essential. It is stuck into the sand to hold your rod when you are not fishing or changing bait.

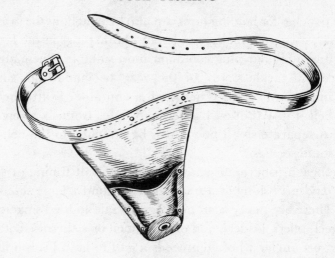

Rod Belt

A rod belt also comes in handy for holding your rod high while bait fishing. Anglers fishing with artificial lures can also use it when reeling in metal squids fast. It will also help to take the strain off your arms and groin when fighting big fish. The type of leather belt with a wide leather backing and deep cup is most suited for surf fishing purposes.

A knife can also be carried in a sheath for instant use. If you can get a good stainless steel knife it will require less care. The other types require constant oiling to prevent rust and cleaning after use. Whatever knife you get it must be sharp at all times.

Other items often needed are cutting and gripping pliers, small oil can, sharpening stone, insect repellent, sun glasses, and a pair of binoculars. The binoculars aren't carried on the beach but can be kept in the car to spot breaking fish or diving birds.

Do you really need all the equipment mentioned above? Well, you may not need every single item on each surf fishing trip, but the sooner you acquire a good basic surf fishing outfit and the necessary accessories, the sooner you will be able to catch fish in the surf. Any surf angler who goes out only partly equipped is operating under a terrific handicap. If you observe the expert or veteran surf anglers in action, you'll notice that almost invariably they have every item required for productive surf fishing.

Chapter 2

Spinning Tackle

If you are just starting to take up surf fishing, you may wonder whether you should get conventional or spinning type surf tackle. Both have their advantages and disadvantages, but if you have a lot of time to go surf fishing and plan to do it often then you can get a conventional surf outfit. You must take your surf fishing seriously, practice often, and become a good caster with conventional tackle or else you'll be plagued by backlashes.

The conventional outfit is also good in rocky areas for big fish. Here you will land more fish with a conventional outfit than with spinning gear. If you plan to do a lot of bait fishing on the bottom with heavy sinkers and baits or use heavy lures to make long casts, you'll also find the conventional outfit more practical. The same applies to fishing spots with strong currents and tides. A conventional outfit will handle the fish much better here than a spin outfit.

Then you may ask, why is it that most of the outfits being used in surf fishing today are spinning rods and reels? The majority of anglers fishing the surf don't get a chance to fish too often and they find a spinning outfit much easier to use. They learn how to cast much sooner and get more distance earlier with a spin outfit than with a conventional one. A spin outfit is lighter, simpler to use, and requires less practice to cast well. It provides more sport with the smaller surf fish and can cast smaller, lighter lures and baits than a conventional outfit.

I would say that your first surf fishing outfit should be a spinning rod and reel. Later on after a year or two, if you find that you can use a conventional outfit for some kinds of surf fishing, then you can get one. In the meantime, however, you can use a spin outfit for most of your surf fishing.

Spinning outfits for surf fishing can also be divided into three classes: light, medium, and heavy. The light surf spinning rod will range from 8 to 9½ ft. in over-all length. This would have a fairly long butt section so that you can use two hands for casting. With such a rod you'll handle mostly the smaller and lighter lures and sinkers weighing from ⅝ oz. up to about 1½ oz.

You can also use a shorter 6½- to 7-ft. spinning rod which has a short handle and is cast with one hand. This is not a true surf rod but is more popular for boat fishing and when fishing in such quiet waters as bays, inlets, and rivers. However, it can also be used in the surf when the water isn't too rough and the fish aren't running too big. In fact, any light spin rod is best suited for short casts, light lures, small fish, and quiet waters. Such short, light spin rods and also bait-casting rods are popular for surf fishing in the shallow waters along the Gulf of Mexico and the west coast of Florida.

The medium surf spinning rod will run from 8½ to 10 ft. in over-all length. The butt section will be anywhere from 18 to 26 in. in length. Such a rod should be able to handle lures from 1 to 2 oz., depending on the action and softness of the tip section. The medium weight spin outfit is fine for open beaches where the surf isn't too strong and the fish don't run too big. This rod will handle a wide range of lures, and can also be used for bait fishing with the smaller, lighter baits and sinkers.

SPINNING SURF ROD

The heavy surf spinning rod, ranging from 9 to 11 ft. in over-all length, will have a butt section anywhere from 20 to 30 in. long. Such a rod will handle lures ranging from 1 to 3 oz. and sinkers up to 3 or 4 oz. This rod is the most practical tool for all-around surf fishing. If you can buy only one spinning rod, then the heavy job is the best one to get. You can still cast fairly light lures with it but can also handle the heavier ones. And if you have to use large baits and sinkers you can do so with the heavy spin rod. Such a rod will do a fair job of handling the larger surf fish in heavy surf and strong currents.

The construction of surf spinning rods varies with the manufacturers. Some come in one piece with just cork grips slipped over the glass blank. Such spinning rods are light and strong but require transporting outside the car. Two-piece rods with a detachable butt section are very popular. All surf rods should have reel seats with screw-threads which hold the reel firmly in place. Sliding rings are not dependable or strong enough for such fishing.

When you buy a surf spinning rod make sure that the guides are wrapped on firmly and have large rings, especially the first gathering guide nearest the butt section. Most surf spinning reels have wide-diameter spools and the line comes off in large coils. Small diameter rings on the guides will shorten your casts. The guides on surf spinning rods should be made of hard metal which can take the wear of the line. Some surf anglers still prefer a tip guide of genuine agate, but hard metal tungsten or carboloy guides do a good job, as well as not cracking like agate guides.

As with conventional rods, the best material for surf spinning rods is fiber glass of hollow construction. Such rods are light but very strong.

The length of a surf spinning rod can be deceiving. An 8½-ft. rod, for example, can be made in light or medium weights, depending on the taper, diameter, and thickness of the glass blank. Most surf spinning rods have a fairly limber tip section and a thick stiff butt section

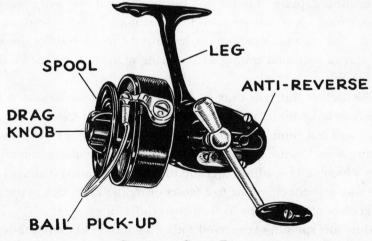

SPOOL   LEG   ANTI-REVERSE   DRAG KNOB   BAIL PICK-UP

SPINNING SURF REEL

which gives them backbone for casting and fighting fish. If the tip is too limber, it won't be able to handle the heavier lures and sinkers; if it's too stiff, it won't cast the lighter lures too well, and can't be used with the lighter spin lines.

If you can find an expert surf angler in your area to recommend a surf spinning rod suitable for your locality, you should follow his advice. Any local tackle dealer who caters to surf anglers and has a good assortment of such tackle can suggest which rod is best suited for the fishing in your waters.

When it comes to surf spinning reels you now have a good assortment to choose from. Here again, find out which ones are being used by the expert surf anglers in your area. In other words, if a large number of anglers swear by a certain make, then you can be sure that it has stood the test of time. The importance does not lie in choosing a domestic model or an imported one, but in being certain that parts and repairs can be obtained if needed.

Surf spinning reels generally come in two sizes—a smaller size which can be used with light or medium rods, and the largest sizes which are used with medium and heavy rods. They vary in the amount of line they hold, but the smaller ones should hold at least 200 to 250 yds. of line while the larger ones generally hold from 250 to 350 yds., depending on the line size.

When you buy a spinning reel make sure it's designed for salt-water fishing, preferably for surf fishing. Such a reel will then have large, strong parts and gears and will be made of non-corrosive materials. Surf spinning reels must be strong enough to take the wear and tear of continual casting and working of lures as well as for fighting big fish.

The friction clutch or drag should be smooth and constant. A drag which jerks or binds will mean broken lines and lost fish because many surf fish come big and take off on fast powerful runs. So when buying a surf spinning reel, make sure it has a smooth dependable drag which can be adjusted gradually. Once adjusted it should stay that way without changing to a looser or tighter drag, unless you turn the knob or other device which changes the setting.

Most surf spinning reels used today have full bail, automatic line pick-ups. They are the most convenient and fastest to use, especially if you plan to do a lot of casting with artificial lures. A spinning reel. which has this pick-up enables you to start the retrieve almost immediately and to be assured that the lure doesn't get a chance to sink and foul in the rocks or seaweed, as often happens if there's a delay in the retrieve. Such a delay often occurs with spinning reels that have manual pick-ups. However, since the manual ones are more dependable, there are fewer parts to go out of order and many surf anglers prefer them. Reels with finger pick-ups are also used but are not too popular since the line may get tangled around the finger or arm. This could easily happen when the wind is blowing, especially at night. Finger pick-ups also bend out of shape if they hit a rock or other obstruction.

The roller over which the line runs when it's being retrieved should be of some hard substance. The continual retrieving of lures and playing of fish will cut grooves in the roller if it is made of poor material. The best ones are made of very hard metal, sapphire, or agate. Some of them are supposed to revolve; if they do, they should turn freely.

Most surf spinning reels also have an anti-reverse lock. When this is in the "on" position it prevents the handle from turning backwards. When in the "off" position the handle will turn both ways, but the angler holds the handle to prevent it from turning backwards. A few anglers leave the anti-reverse on while casting and retrieving, but most fish with the anti-reverse off until a fish is hooked, then it is thrown on. Some reels have an automatic anti-reverse which takes over as soon as a fish is hooked. The anti-reverse is a big help in case your hand slips off the reel handle or you have to remove the hand to grab or gaff a fish. It is also handy when bait-fishing on the bottom, changing lures or baits, and moving from one spot to another.

Another thing to check when buying a surf spinning reel is the handle knob. This should be big and easy to grab and hold, but you should be certain that it doesn't wear too quickly. Some spinning reels have plastic knobs which revolve directly on a metal shaft, causing the plastic knob to wear and get loose. The result is replacement, which often means buying a whole new handle. A good reel handle will have a metal bushing so that there is a minimum of wear at this point.

The closed-spool or "American" type spinning reel is also used in surf fishing. These reels are very popular with fresh-water fishermen, and there are many of these smaller models to choose from. Manufacturers now make reels that are used by surf anglers for salt-water fishing. The closed-spool reel gets its name from the fact that the spool holding the line is enclosed within a cover (usually cone-shaped) containing a hole through which the line emerges. On an open-spool type reel the line leaves the spool in wide spirals or coils, thus requiring a rod to have large guides—especially the first or "gathering" guide. A closed-spool reel, however, permits the line to leave in a straight line and can be used with a rod having small guides. The main advantages of a closed-spool reel is that it's very easy to use and gives less trouble on windy days and at night. Most closed-spool reels have less casting distance and hold less line than open-type reels. Another bad feature is that there are more points of friction and wear

Surf spinning tackle has slowly but surely been replacing conventional outfits in the surf. Shown is Dick Wolff, who has helped popularize spinning.

on closed-spool reels. The line rubs against these points and is often weakened. Also, more time is needed to change spools on closed-type reels. However, these disadvantages are overlooked by many surf anglers who prefer the ease with which they can use the closed-spool type reel.

In fact, the main advantage of any spinning reel, whether it's an open- or closed-type, is casting efficiency. You don't have to spend valuable hours, days, or even months learning how to cast. In a matter of minutes, or at most an hour or two, you can cast long distances with spin reels—and without being bothered by backlashes. You are soon left free to concentrate on using the baits and lures and on locating and hooking the fish.

Spinning lines used in surf fishing come either in braided nylon, braided dacron, or monofilament nylon. The braided nylon or dacron lines have never become too popular for surf fishing when used with spin rods and reels for they do not stand up too well around rocks, reefs, mussels, and barnacles. Because braided lines also tend to fray and wear more readily from continuous casting or friction, most spin casters fishing the surf use monofilament nylon.

Monofilament nylon lines—thin, waterproof, tough, and almost invisible—cast smoothly and give good distance. Most of the monofilament lines on the market today are made from Dupont nylon and are called "Tynex." Each line manufacturer uses the same raw material and processes it, dyes it, and labels it under his trade name. It's the same basic product with slight differences in diameter, stretch, limpness, hardness, and so on, depending on what is done to the line. Since any of the reputable line companies puts out a good product, you could try a few until you find one which suits you.

Nylon monofilament lines come in various tests from light, thin lines that test a fraction of a pound up to 100 lbs. or more. For surf fishing you'll use mostly lines testing 8, 10, 12, 15, or 18 lbs. Occasionally, you may want to use a 20- or 25-lb. test line with a heavy spin rod to make short casts for big fish, but lines testing 12 and 15 lbs. are most practical for all-around surf fishing. These are the tests which can be used with a medium weight surf spinning outfit for most surf fishing.

Most of the accessories covered in the previous chapter on conventional tackle will also be needed when using spin outfits: waders or boots, waterproof jacket, pistol belt, shoulder bag or pouches and plug containers, stringer, knife, and gaff. The gaff is even more important for the spin angler than the man who uses conventional tackle. A surf angler with a conventional outfit can often lift or drag a good-sized fish when beaching him. But the angler using a spin outfit will need a gaff to help him in the final stages of the battle.

Chapter 3

Casting

If you have a conventional surf fishing outfit with a revolving spool reel the first important step in using it is to fill the reel spool properly with line. The best way to do this is to attach your reel to the rod and then run the line through the guides and tie the end of it to the reel spool. Should you have a two-piece surf rod you can just attach your reel to the butt section if you want. The next step after tying the end of the line to the reel spool is to place your spools of line next to each other and slide them on a pencil, stick, or iron rod. Make sure that the spools of line are in the proper sequence so that the line will come off the right way. However, this won't concern you unless you buy four or six 50-yard spools. Most manufacturers also sell surf lines on one large spool holding 200 or 250 yds. of line. Here you merely place the spool on a stick or rod and reel it off on the reel spool.

The important thing to remember is that the line should be packed on the reel spool not too loose or too tight. The person who holds the line spools should press against the sides to provide the proper tension; however, if you must do this alone you can hold the line between the fingers of the left hand as you wind it on the reel with your right.

When the line reaches a point about one-quarter of an inch from the bar supports on your reel, you have enough line on the reel. If you put on anymore, you'll find that when it spools unevenly it will rub against the bars on the reel. You must make allowance for extra space in advance. If the reel spool is only one-half or two-thirds full, you'll have trouble casting and won't get much distance.

After the reel is properly filled and the rod is rigged, you are ready to cast. If possible, go down to the beach or along any body of water to practice casting. For this, a sinker about 3 or 4 oz. is best to use to get the feel of the weight, because a light sinker or lure is more difficult to cast in the beginning.

The first step in surf casting with the conventional rod is the proper

When casting with a conventional rod and reel, one should spread his feet well apart, as illustrated here.

stance. On a sandy beach, you stand with the legs well apart, face down the beach to the right, and point your left foot down the beach. In this position your chest faces more or less to the right.

Now throw your reel into free-spool and let out about 3 ft. of line from the tip of your rod. Grasp the rod butt right under the reel and press your thumb against the line or reel spool. Some surf anglers like to cast with the thumb against the side of the reel spool whereas others keep their thumb on the line itself. With your left hand gripping the end of the butt, you raise the rod so that it is about shoulder high (see page 22). The face of your reel (the side with the handle) will point toward the ground.

In a casting position, you now bring with a quick motion the rod tip over your head. This is done by pushing forward with your right hand and pulling back with your left (see page 22). Your torso twists to face the target, the rod tip passes a point directly over your head, and, when you feel it bend (see page 23), you remove your thumb from the reel spool. As the line starts to run out you put the thumb back on the spool to feel the line running out under your thumb. Keep it there at all times, applying a bit more pressure if it runs too fast. When the sinker or lure reaches a point just above the target, you stop the cast by pressing down with your thumb (see page 23).

The whole secret of good casting is timing and thumbing. You must practice until you know just when to release the line from under your thumb, and you must get the feel of the reel spool or line moving out at the proper speed. Too much or too sudden pressure will cause the sinker to fall a short distance away; too little pressure will allow the line to move off too fast and will result in a backlash also shortening the cast.

Because another difficulty arises when spooling the line on the retrieve, it should be put back on the reel spool as evenly as possible. If it bunches up in the middle or at one end you can have trouble on the next cast. The right way to spool the line is to let it run between the thumb and forefinger of your left hand just above the reel. As you reel in, work your two fingers back and forth guiding the line evenly on the reel spool. There are now surf reels with level winding devices on the market which will help to do this.

The cast described above is the basic overhead cast which can be used from the sand beaches or from jetties or when wading out in the water. However, you may have to shorten the line from the lure to rod tip, depending on obstructions behind you and space you have for the cast. Whenever possible try to get up on a rock or other height which gives you more room behind and below to get power leverage into the cast.

In the beginning, the achievement of smoothness and accuracy is more important than that of distance. Most surf fish will be caught fairly close to the beach anyway, so later on when you have mastered the casting techniques, you can try to heave it out as far as possible.

Most of your casts will be overhead casts, but at times you may have to make a side cast in which the rod tip travels almost parallel to the ground. If this cast is done with a fast snap the lure will take off like a bullet. It is a good cast to use against a strong wind but certainly not on a crowded beach or jetty. To offset a tendency to cast sideways, even when an overhead cast is being done, it's important for the beginner to practice casting directly overhead as much as possible. The rod tip will travel toward the right anyway, so keep it overhead as much as you can in order to be a safe caster when among other surf fishermen.

The same casting techniques and positions described above can be used with a spin rod and reel. Start the cast directly behind you.

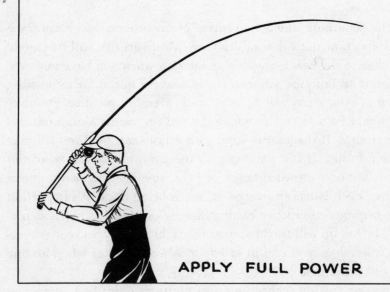

CASTING WITH
CONVENTIONAL TACKLE

START OF CAST

APPLY FULL POWER

REMOVE THUMB
FROM SPOOL

END OF CAST

CASTING WITH
SPINNING TACKLE

START OF CAST

APPLY FULL POWER

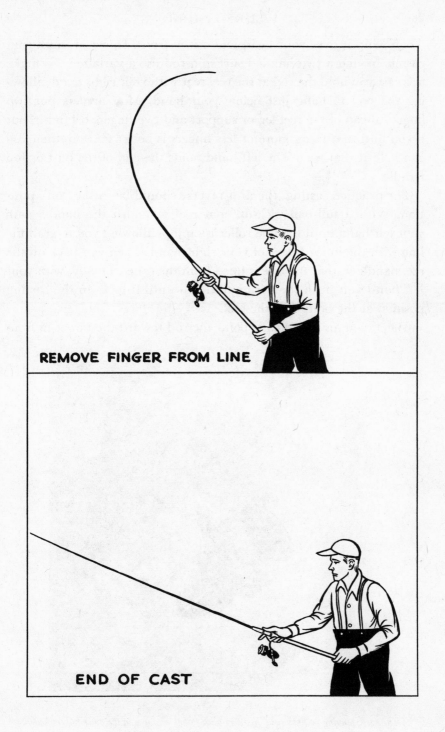

REMOVE FINGER FROM LINE

END OF CAST

Then whip it over your head and out in front. However, most spin casters having a two-handed surf spin rod use a variation. To make this cast you hold the rod at the reel seat with your right hand, allowing the reel to hang just below your hand. Most anglers put two fingers ahead of the reel leg or support and two fingers behind it, but if you find that using more or less fingers is better for you, then you can hold it that way. The left hand holds the end of the butt or rod handle.

For practice casting, the anti-reverse should be in the "off" position. With a full-bail pick-up spin reel you turn the handle with your left hand until the line roller is on top, allowing you to grab the line with the index finger of your right hand. Then you back off the reel handle so that the line is freed from the roller. Finally, with your left hand you push the wire bail down until it locks in the casting position at the bottom of the reel.

When you are set to cast, point the rod toward the target in front

The surf spinning outfit is held this way with thumb on top and the other fingers below.

of you at about the 10 o'clock position on a clock (see page 24). Next you bring your rod back sharply over your head until it drops behind you to about the 2 o'clock position (see page 24). Then as the lure or sinker bends the rod into a big arc, you start the forward cast by pushing with your right hand and pulling back with your left (see page 25). When the rod reaches the original 10 o'clock position in front of you, release the line and the weight will sail out over the target (see page 25). When it reaches a spot almost directly above the target, you stop the cast by dropping your index finger to the lip of the reel spool, or you turn the reel handle forward with your left hand.

To cast smoothly, correct timing in releasing your line and the motions involved is also required. If you release the line too soon, it will sail high into the air; however, if you are too late, the lure will drop in front of you a short distance away.

One way to get this timing and feel of the rod and weight is to go through the same motions as described but not to release the line from your finger. In other words, you just wave the rod back and forth in the casting motions without releasing the line. You will feel the rod tip bend under the weight of the sinker and lure. After doing this several times, you can try releasing the line from your right index finger at the proper moment.

It would help if you could watch experienced surf anglers casting with either conventional or spinning rods, depending on which one you have. If you can get one of these men to show you how it's done, he can show you the proper procedure and point out any mistakes you are making.

However, most surf anglers learn to cast without such guidance, and if they practice sufficiently they soon learn how to cast far enough to catch fish in the surf.

Chapter 4

Lures

It wasn't too long ago that a surf angler carried only one or two kinds of artificial lures. Then gradually more and more lures were developed for surf fishing and today the well-equipped surf angler is loaded down with a variety of lures.

The metal squid was one of the first lures used in surf fishing, and today it is still popular and productive in the surf. Metal squids come in many shapes, sizes, and weights for surf fishing, starting from tiny ½-oz. models for light spin rods up to 4 or 5 oz. for use with heavy conventional surf rods.

Most metal squids are supposed to represent small baitfish. The small, narrow types imitate sand eels or silversides while the larger, broader ones simulate the herrings, shiners, anchovies, mullet, and menhaden. Metal squids are molded from block tin, lead, or other metals, but the best ones are usually made from block tin with a bit of lead added to prevent cracking. These have a silvery finish which doesn't tarnish so readily whereas all-lead squids soon turn black, so many anglers paint them white or yellow. Many metal squids are also chrome-plated.

Two basic types of metal squids are made: one has a stationary or fixed hook which is imbedded in the body of the lure, while the other type has a swinging hook which is attached to the metal squid with a pin, eye, or ring. Both types are equally good. The swinging hook type has a somewhat wider sweeping action and is less easily thrown by a hooked fish, mainly because the fish cannot get any leverage.

Although the plain, unadorned metal squid will catch fish, most anglers add either strips of pork rind or tie feathers or bucktail around the hook. The most popular colors in feathers or bucktail are white, yellow, red, or combinations of these.

Metal squids of various kinds can be bought in most coastal fishing tackle stores. However, since these lures are often lost, many surf

METAL SQUIDS

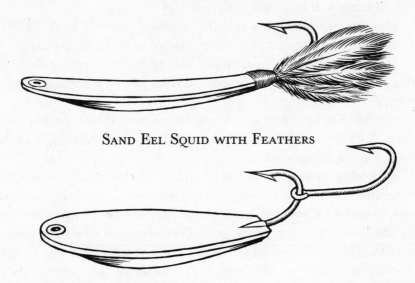

SAND EEL SQUID WITH FEATHERS

MULLET SQUID WITH SECOND HOOK

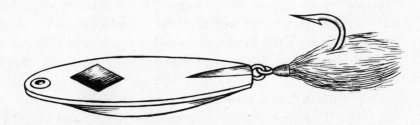

SAND EEL SQUID WITH PORK RIND AND TAIL HOOK

MULLET SQUID WITH SWING HOOK AND BUCKTAIL

anglers prefer to make their own metal squids. Details on how they can be made will be found in Chapter 14.

Most metal squids have a better action if they are bent slightly. Sometimes a double bend is made instead of just a single curve. A little experimenting by casting and reeling the metal squid through the water and watching its action will show just how much of a bend it needs.

Metal squids should be kept shiny by polishing them with fine steel wool. At the beach you can shine a metal squid which is dull by rubbing it in the damp sand.

Somewhat similar to the metal squids are the spoons which are sometimes used in surf fishing. Although some of the larger spoons can be cast with conventional outfits, they are better when used in the smaller sizes with spinning gear. They also come in a wide variety of sizes, weights, shapes, and finishes. For surf fishing use the longer, thicker, narrower types of spoons. Plain spoons will take fish, but those with a strip of pork rind added or with feathers or bucktail attached seem to work best. Spoons for surf fishing should be the salt-water models because they have stronger hooks and fittings, such as split-rings. On the best ones, the split-rings are soldered so that they won't open when a large fish is hooked.

When surf anglers discovered back in the 1930's that plugs would take many fish and especially striped bass, they started a clamor for these lures which has never ceased. Today you'll find on the market a wide variety of wooden and plastic plugs, most of which can be used in surf fishing.

To simplify matters we can separate plugs into two classes: the "surface" plugs and the "underwater" types. Surface plugs, as the name implies, stay on the surface of the water, although few of them may dive under a few inches when reeled fast or when caught by a wave or the current. But most were designed to stay on top throughout the retrieve.

One of the earliest surface plugs used in surf fishing was the "flap-tail" type. This plug, which comes in different sizes and weights, has a small metal spoon attached to the tail. When it is reeled through the water, the spoon revolves and flutters, causing a disturbance behind it. The flaptail was originated by James Heddon's Sons and is still sold by them. Fishermen consider it a killer for striped bass, especially in the fall of the year when mullet are found swimming near the surface. It is still a good lure to use at times.

Another surface type is the "popping" plug, which has a cupped head or slanted head. Creating a commotion on top of the water and a big splash when jerked, it can also simulate an injured mullet or other baitfish. Popping plugs are made in different sizes from small 1-oz. models for the lightest spin rods to big, 4-oz. jobs for the conventional rods.

Another group of surface plugs are the "swimming" types. Equipped with a metal lip which makes them wriggle from side to side as they move on top of the water, they create a ripple and a wake when reeled steadily and also a splash when jerked. The Striper Atom is a good example of this type. It comes in various sizes and weights.

Somewhat similar is the big "jointed-eel" plug, which also has a metal lip and may be 14 in. long in the largest size. This plug also swims on top in a snaky action if reeled slowly. A fine example of this plug, which has a good record as a big striped bass killer, is the Giant Pikie made by Creek Chub Bait Co.

Another plug which can be worked on or near the surface is the "darter" type. When reeled slowly or twitched, it works on the surface creating a ripple or wake; however, when jerked or reeled fast, it travels in a zig-zag darting fashion just below the surface like a frightened baitfish. Some fine darters for surf fishing are made by Stan Gibbs Lures.

In the underwater types, one of the earliest models used in the surf is the well-known "wobbler" plug. The original, called the "Bass-Oreno" and made by South Bend Tackle Co., has been on the market for many years as a fresh-water favorite. The salt-water models naturally are heavier and have stronger hooks.

The largest group of underwater plugs are the metal lip types which wriggle when reeled in and come in one piece or jointed. The Creek Chub Pikies are a good example, but many other companies make similar types which also take fish.

Of course, numerous plugs on the market which can't be covered in detail here are also good. You'll find that most of them will fall into the classes or types mentioned above; in fact, when buying plugs

PLUGS

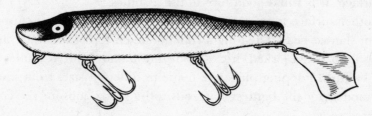

FLAPTAIL

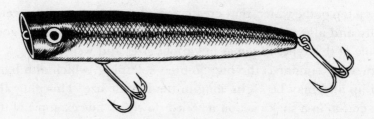

POPPER

SURFACE SWIMMER

JOINTED EEL

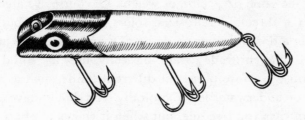

WOBBLER

DARTER

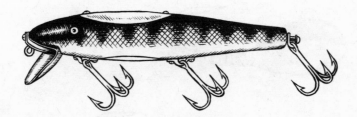

SMALL UNDERWATER

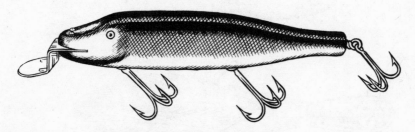

LARGE UNDERWATER

care must be taken not to duplicate those you already have. In other
words, if you already have two or three darter types, you don't need
others of the same size, color, or weight. Of course, it's a good idea to
have two or three different sizes, colors, and weights, but don't end
up buying a dozen darters made by as many companies just because
they have different trade names. Basically, they are still darter types
and if you buy more plugs get different kinds, such as swimmers,
poppers, or underwater jobs. Naturally, you should have a duplicate
of each in case you lose one, but when it comes to plugs it's best to
have a mixed assortment of the different types.

Plugs are made from either wood or plastic, although there are
now more of the latter. Both materials are good, except that the plastic
ones have more permanent colors, stand up better from continual
banging around, and are more standard in weight.

When it comes to colors, it is best to try to match the baitfish on
which the fish are feeding at the time. Since most salt-water baitfish
have blue or green backs, silvery sides, and white bellies, plugs in
these natural finishes are usually best. Red and white, all silver, or all

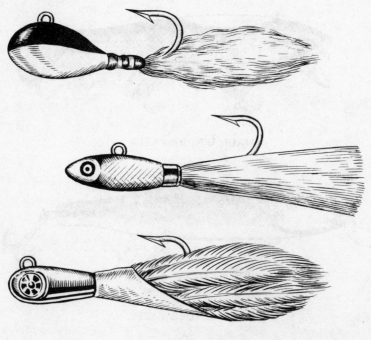

JIGS

yellow plugs are also good for surf fishing. If you are trying to imitate an eel, plugs with brown, grey, or purple are fine.

One important thing to keep in mind when buying plugs is to be sure they are made for salt-water fishing. Those made for fresh-water fishing will catch fish, of course, but they are usually too light for casting and the hooks are too weak to handle big fish. Even salt-water plugs often have hooks that are too weak, because the best hooks will eventually rust and weaken.

One lure that is becoming more and more popular in surf fishing is the so-called jig, also known as the bucktail, bugeye, bullhead, or barracuda. Even though they are especially good to use with spin tackle in the smaller sizes, the very largest can be cast and used with conventional surf tackle. Jigs come in different weights, colors, sizes, and dressings, but a similarity lies in having a heavy metal head with feathers or bucktail or nylon or rubber or plastic skirts wrapped around the hook. The metal head is either chromed or painted in various colors, with the white and yellow heads being used mostly in salt-water fishing. The effectiveness of plain chrome or silver heads is based on the fact that they are probably mistaken for tiny baitfish, but jigs also can be made to represent shrimp or small crabs in the water.

Jigs will range in weight from small ½-oz. models up to 3 or 4 oz. for surf fishing. A single hook is usually molded into the head of the jig, and these run from No. 1 hooks in the smaller jigs to 8/0 or larger in the big ones.

A good assortment of jigs in different colors and weights should be carried by surf anglers. They don't take up much room and can often mean the difference between fish and no fish in the surf, especially in southern waters. Jigs are very deadly here for a wide variety of species, but they will also take fish in northern waters and are especially effective for the smaller school stripers, bluefish, mackerel, and similar species. Jigs can be reeled fast near the surface of the water to simulate a frantic baitfish, or they can be reeled slowly and bounced on the bottom to imitate a shrimp or other small crustaceans.

One of the best lures which can be used for large striped bass is the rigged eel, although it will also take bluefish and occasionally other fish. Actually, the whole rigged eel is not an artificial lure but a natural bait. However, it is used like an artificial lure—sufficient reason for including it in this section.

You can catch your own live eels by using eel pots baited with dead fish, small baitfish, crushed clams, or crabs and set out in bays or creeks where eels abound. You can also buy live or frozen eels from bait dealers, fish markets, or tackle stores. The size of eel will depend on the tackle: small ones from 8 to 12 in. for spin outfits; larger ones from 12 to 18 in. for conventional surf rods.

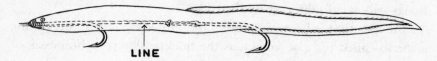

LINE

METHOD OF RIGGING AN EEL

There are dozens of ways to rig an eel. Here is one method to produce a rigged eel which will take plenty of punishment. First you make or get a long 12- or 14-in. needle (a long upholsterer's needle will serve the purpose). Or you can make your own by using a thin metal wire or rod. It should have a point on one end and an eye or slot on the other. Next you get some 7/0, 8/0, or 9/0 hooks, depending on the size of the eel—the larger the eel, the larger the hooks. Even smaller hooks can be used with spinning size eels. O'Shaughnessy hooks are usually used but some anglers prefer the Eagle Claw pattern. Then you need some strong linen or nylon fish line testing at least 45 lbs. and also some fine brass or copper wire.

The first step in rigging an eel is to tie about 18 in. of the heavy line to the eye of the needle. Next tie one of the hooks to the other end and insert the needle into the underside of the eel at the vent. Push the needle through the eel inside the belly until it emerges from the mouth then pull on the needle until the line also comes out of the eel's mouth. Thus the hook is buried inside the eel by pulling on the line. Double back the needle and push the point into the eel's mouth and force it out at the neck, or about 2 in. from the eel's nose. Pull the needle out through this hole made at the eel's neck and untie the needle from the line. This leaves a loop of line protruding from the eel's mouth and the end of the line emerges from the eel's neck. Now tie another hook to the end of this line and pull the hook shank inside the eel—this should leave a few inches of line protruding from the eel's mouth in a loop.

The next step is to take about 4 or 5 in. of the thin flexible wire and run one end into the eel's mouth and out the gill opening on one side. Then pull more wire out this opening over the top of the eel's head and push the end through the gill opening on the opposite side of the head. Force this wire out through the eel's mouth. This acts as a bridle, and the final step is to tie the two ends of wire protruding from the eel's mouth around the loop of line several times. You can use the eel as is or you can put a barrel swivel into the loop. Some anglers also tie some line around the eel where the hooks emerge to reinforce them.

This sounds somewhat complicated and difficult, but in reality it is simple and takes little time. If you have another method and find it suitable, you can of course use it instead. But the method of rigging outlined here has been well tested over the years.

Although the rigged eel works fairly well with nothing else attached, many surf anglers also rig eels with various gadgets to give them weight or action. Some take a small metal squid and attach it at the head of the eel. Others make special metal lips which are attached to give the eels a lively action. Still other anglers like eel bobs or eel-tails. Here the head of the eel is removed and a lead weight is inserted under the skin to provide the weight. All of these variations have taken fish, and which is best is a matter of personal preference. There is one advantage in a weighted eel besides action: it provides more weight for casting farther and against a wind.

The skin from an eel is used with many lures for surf fishing. These eelskin lures have weighted heads to which the skin (turned inside out) is tied. Most of them have holes in the metal heads to permit water to enter and inflate the skin. One or two hooks are attached to the heads by means of chains, cables, or steel leader wire. The heads come in various sizes, shapes and weights. Since they sink fast, these eelskin lures are especially effective when used in inlets, canals, and

METAL RING
SOLDERED TO SQUID

EELSKIN SQUID

other places where the water is fast and deep. It is a very effective lure in the Cape Cod Canal in Massachusetts.

Some surf anglers also solder a ring to a metal squid and tie an eelskin around the ring, thus giving the skin a snaky action. Since the front part of the metal squid is uncovered the shiny metal also acts as an attractor.

Still other surf anglers, especially in New England, take an eelskin and pull it over a metal squid to cover it completely. Then they tie the skin in front of the lure to keep it in place. Somewhat similar is the idea of pulling an eelskin over a wooden or plastic plug. To do this all the hooks must be removed, then replaced outside the skin.

Finally, we have such combination lures as the "splasher" rig, where a section of broomstick or dowel (depending on the weight you want) is used. This wooden splasher, which can be anywhere from 2 to 5 in. long, has a screw eye on each end or a wire running through the middle with eyes fashioned at each end. The end of the line is attached to one eye while an 18- to 24-inch nylon or cable wire leader is attached to the other eye. At the end of this leader you can use a small streamer fly, jig, or small spoon. The idea is to cast out and reel or jerk the rig in slowly, causing a commotion or splash with the big wooden float. The lure itself is just behind and traveling close to the surface like a small baitfish or shrimp. This lure is especially effective for small stripers, bluefish, pollock, and mackerel.

A somewhat similar method is to use a surface plug and, about 20 to 24 in. ahead of it on the leader, to attach a short 6- to 8-in. dropper with a hook and a strip of pork rind. This double lure also makes the plug act as an attractor while the pork rind travels just ahead and below. Sometimes the fish will strike the plug, but more often they go for the pork rind strip.

In mentioning pork rind, I should advise that it's a good idea to take along a couple of jars of the tough pigskin. The strips can be added to the hooks of plugs, metal squids, jigs, spoons, and other lures. The same thing can also be done with strips of squid bait.

Before we leave the lures, it may be a good idea to explain the best way to attach them to the end of the line. First, regardless of whether you use a conventional surf rod or spinning tackle, you should either double your line for several feet or attach some kind of leader to take the shock of casting and rubbing against obstructions, as well as to take the strain of landing or beaching a fish. Nylon leader material works fine for such a leader. For the spin rod the leader should be a few pounds heavier in test than the main line. With a conventional rod it can be the same test or a bit heavier.

At the end of this leader you should tie a snap-swivel for a quick change of lures. One of the best snaps on the market for this purpose is the stainless steel one made by Pompanette Products. Some surf anglers attach their lures directly to this snap. Although this works fairly well, you man run into trouble when you hook such sharp-toothed fish as bluefish, barracuda, or fish with sharp gills like snook. Other fish can cut a leader or line with their dorsal fins. So it's a good idea to attach short wire leaders anywhere from 6 to 10 in. long to each lure. Stainless steel wire of various thicknesses can be obtained to make such short leaders. The thin wire is best for small, light lures while the heavier wire is used for the larger lures. After some practice, you can twist loops on both ends of the wire leader with round-nosed pliers very neatly. One loop will, of course, go through the eye of the lure while the other one will fit into the snap on the end of the line.

Chapter 5

Natural Baits

When artificial lures fail to produce fish in the surf, the angler often turns to natural baits. There are some surf anglers who, scoffing at bait fishermen, take pride in the fact that they always use artificial lures. However, they often miss out on some good fishing because, if they want to catch such fish as channel bass, summer or winter flounders, blackfish or tautog, kinfish, or whiting, they must use natural baits for best results. Then there are many days when such gamefish as striped bass, bluefish, and weakfish prefer the natural bait to the artificial.

Then again, bait fishing in the surf is a very relaxing, restful form of fishing. It is less tiring than squidding with artificials. Since the angler who uses both bait and artificials during the season will end up with more fish, we'll cover the most popular baits used in the surf here.

BLOODWORMS

These are the round, smooth-bodied pink worms which are also known as white worms and beak throwers. They get the latter name because when handled they shoot out a long proboscis armed with four tiny black jaws or "beaks." Two kinds of bloodworms are found along the Atlantic Coast from Canada to the Carolinas. They live on the tidal mud flats where they can be dug at low tide with a garden fork or clam rake. Bloodworms are also sold by many bait and tackle dealers. Although these worms may be found along the Pacific Coast, they are not too numerous there and are flown from the East to supply the demand. Small pieces of bloodworms make good bait for kingfish (whiting), porgies or scup, and blackfish or tautog, but whole worms can be used for weakfish and summer flounders. Several whole bloodworms on a hook make a top bait for striped bass. On the Pacific Coast they are used for croakers and surf perches.

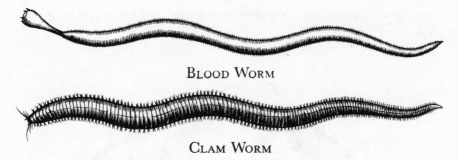

BLOOD WORM

CLAM WORM

CLAMWORMS

The clamworms—or sandworms, as they are often called—differ from bloodworms in that they are flatter and have a dark green or blueish back and red or orange undersides. They also have visible segments and appendages or "legs" along the sides. Clamworms, often found on the same tidal flats as bloodworms, lie deeper in the mud than bloodworms, so you often have to dig twice in the same spot to reach them. Clamworms are found along the Atlantic Coast from Canada to New Jersey. Along the Pacific, where they are called mussel worms or pile worms, they are found from Alaska to San Diego. You can buy clamworms from bait dealers or tackle stores. Along the Atlantic Coast clamworms are used for weakfish, striped bass, winter and summer flounders, blackfish or tautog, and northern whiting. Along the Pacific they will take corbina, spotfin and yellowfin croakers, and surf perches.

SURF CLAM

The big surf or "skimmer" clam is a popular bait for surf fishing. These clams live in the sand along the Atlantic ocean beaches from the shore to deeper water offshore. They dig into the sand and lie partly exposed. If you wade in the shallow water up to a few feet in the surf you can often see them and dig them out for bait. They are often found washed up high and dry on the beaches at low tide, especially after storms and heavy seas. Surf clams are also sold by many bait dealers and coastal tackle stores and can be kept on ice or in a cool spot for several days.

The whole insides of a surf clam can be used for such fish as striped bass and channel bass. Smaller pieces are used for many other surf fish.

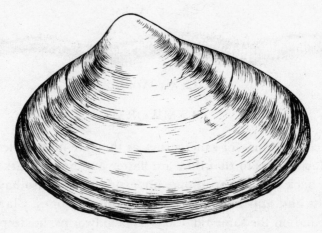

SURF CLAM

BLUE CRAB

This is the bay crab which is found along most of the Atlantic Coast, sold in fish markets, and served in restaurants. The "soft-shelled" and "shedder" stages of the blue crab make the best bait. Crabs molt or shed their hard coverings as they grow. A shedder or peeler crab has reached the state where it is ready to cast off its hard shell soon, at which time it is called a soft-shell crab. Both kinds make good bait. The soft-shell crab can be used as is, but the shedder or peeler crab still has its hard covering which must be removed before using.

Blue crabs in soft-shelled or shedder stages are sometimes sold by bait dealers. Fish markets, of course, carry soft crabs. But they are pretty expensive so many surf anglers catch their own. This can be done in many salt-water bays by wading in shallow water and scooping up the crabs with a long-handled crab net. Most of the crabs you will catch will be hard-shelled ones, and these can be kept for eating. Every once in a while you'll get a soft-shell or shedder crab, which can be kept in moist seaweed and later transferred to a cool spot.

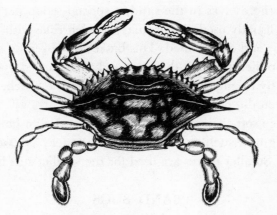

BLUE CRAB

When using the crabs, hook and tie a whole one on a large hook if you are seeking striped bass, channel bass, or big weakfish. If you are after smaller weakfish, kingfish, croakers, or similar-sized fish, use a whole claw, leg, or piece of meat from the body.

LADY CRAB

This crab is also called the calico and sand crab. Found along the sandy beaches from Cape Cod to the Gulf of Mexico, they often steal the bait from surf fishermen. But they also make good bait when small or in the soft-shell or shedder stages. Lady crabs can often be caught with the same long-handled crab nets used for blue crabs. Since they

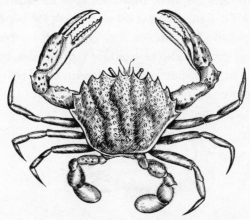

LADY CRAB

often bury themselves in the sand, a special scoop net with a rake attached is usually used. An ordinary garden rake with a small wire basket at the end can be used. This basket is hooked on so that when the rake is pulled through the sand and then turned over, the crabs fall into it. By raking through the sand along the beaches at low tide you can often dig out enough lady crabs for bait.

The whole soft-shelled or shedder lady crab can be placed on a hook for big fish, such as striped bass, channel bass, weakfish, and similar fish. Smaller pieces are used for the smaller surf fish.

SAND BUGS

These bugs are also called beach bugs, sand crabs, and mole crabs. Some call them sand fleas, but they are much larger than the true ones. Sand bugs are easily recognized by oval-shaped bodies that look like tiny eggs. They are smooth on top and have legs underneath with which they can bury themselves in the wet sand along the surf. Most numerous right under the breaking waves, sand bugs are found along both the Atlantic and Pacific coasts. You can catch them by probing with your hands in the wet sand as a wave recedes. However, if you want to catch large quantities in a short time you can use a scoop trap made from wire mesh. This has a long handle and is dragged against a receding wave so that the sand bugs are washed into the trap.

Sand bugs can be kept alive in a cool spot for quite some time. When using them for bait, put several on a hook for big fish and one or two for smaller fish. They make very good bait for pompano and blackfish or tautog but can also be used for striped bass, channel bass, black drum, corbina, and spotfin and yellowfin croakers. Just run the hook through them once from the undersides and out the back.

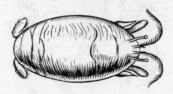

SAND BUG

SHRIMP

There are many kinds of shrimp which can be used in surf fishing, the most common being the large jumbo or edible shrimp which are sold in most fish markets. Here you get just the tails with the meat, and after peeling them you have a good bait which can be used for weakfish, channel bass, kingfish, and other surf fish.

In warmer waters you can obtain live shrimp either by netting them at night with a light or buying them from a bait dealer. These are somewhat smaller species and are usually used whole and alive on the hook. However, if they are not available alive you can also use them dead. Shrimp are hooked through the back or tail and will catch weakfish or sea trout, channel bass or drum, black drum, pompano, snook, and flounders.

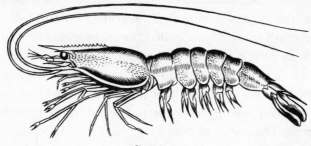

Shrimp

MULLET

These silver baitfish are often used in surf fishing, especially from North Carolina south to Florida and the Gulf of Mexico. However, they are also found in northern waters and can be used there for many fish. Two kinds of mullet—the smaller "silver" mullet and the larger "striped" mullet—are generally found in the surf. You can catch your own mullet if you have a long seine and locate a school in shallow water near shore. A cast net is even better if you know how to use it. Mullet generally come closer to shore at night and that is the best time to catch them. You can buy them from any bait dealers and in fish markets.

Mullet will not stay alive for long so they should be kept on ice or frozen until used. The smaller ones are used whole for such fish as

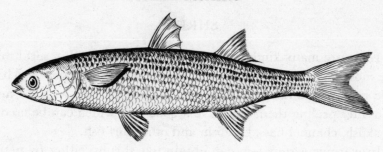

MULLET

striped bass, channel bass, snook, tarpon, and sharks. The larger mullet are filleted or cut into chunks and used for the same fish as well as
for almost any gamefish that is found in the surf.

MENHADEN

This baitfish is right behind the mullet in popularity when it comes
to surf bottom fishing. Often called the mossbunker or "bunker" for
short, it is an oily, flat, deep-bodied member of the herring family.
There are several species of menhaden found in the Atlantic and Gulf
of Mexico. Millions of pounds of these fish are caught by commercial
fishermen with purse seines to be processed into oil, fertilizer, and
animal feeds. Thousands of pounds are also used for chumming when
boat fishing for bluefish and tuna. Surf anglers can buy fresh or frozen
menhaden from bait dealers. Sometimes caught when they come close
to shore, most menhaden average about a foot in length. After you
get the menhaden, keep them frozen or on ice at all times because
they spoil quickly, especially in hot weather.

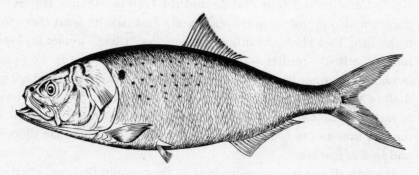

MENHADEN

The small menhaden up to about 6 in. or so can be used whole on the hook for such fish as striped bass, bluefish, channel bass, and other big fish. The larger menhaden must be cut into chunks or filleted and cut into strips. Besides the fish mentioned above, menhaden will also take weakfish, summer flounder, rays, sharks, and many other surf fish.

SQUID

The natural squid makes a very good bait for many fish found in the surf. These cousins of the octopus are usually found swimming offshore in deeper, colder waters where they are caught commercially for food and bait. Sometimes they come close to shore, usually at night, and can be caught with dip nets or on treble hooks baited with small fish. However, you can usually obtain them in fish markets or from bait and tackle dealers. A whole squid makes a top bait for big striped bass, but smaller ones can be used for big weakfish and channel bass. Strips can be used for small weakfish, bluefish, summer flounder, and kingfish. You can keep squid on ice or freeze them for future use, although some anglers cut them into strips and put them in a jar with salt brine.

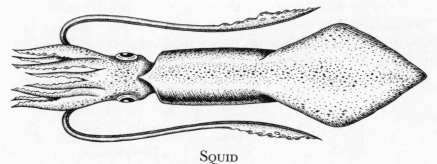

Squid

OTHER BAITFISH

Surf anglers also use other baitfish at times, such as herring, sardines, anchovies, sand-eels, spearing or silversides, and killifish. Larger fish, such as mackerel, bonito, porgies, and blue runners, can also be cut up and used for bait. One of the best baits for bluefish in the surf is the butterfish, which will also take striped bass at times. Live eels also are taken by striped bass if they are fished over sandy bottoms where they can't hide or foul your rig.

BOTTOM RIGS

The surf angler who uses natural baits must know how to make up rigs for this fishing. Such sinkers as the round and bank types for rocky areas and pyramid types for sandy beaches are needed. Sinkers weighing 2 or 3 oz. will suffice when used with spinning tackle, but conventional tackle requires sinkers weighing from 4 to 6 oz. You'll also need barrel swivels, three-way swivels, and fish-finders for making up rigs plus coils of nylon leader material in various pound tests, such as 20-, 30-, and 40-lb. The lighter nylon is used with spinning tackle and for small fish, while the heavier material is used with conventional tackle and for bigger fish. Stainless steel wire material is also needed for sharp-toothed fish, such as bluefish and sharks. Finally you'll need loose hooks in various sizes from No. 1 up to 9/0. The O'Shaughnessy pattern has been a favorite for many years, but the Eagle Claw type is also widely used for surf bottom fishing.

The basic surf fishing rig is the "standard surf rig" which makes use of a three-way swivel. The sinker is tied on a short length of line to one eye of the swivel, and a leader with a hook is tied to another eye. This leader can be nylon, cable wire, or stainless steel wire and can vary in length according to the fishing being done. Usually about 18 in. is right for most surf fishing. Finally, the line from the reel is tied to the remaining eye.

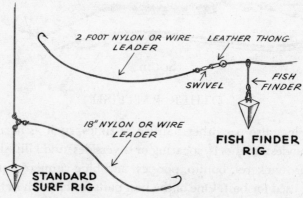

BOTTOM FISHING RIGS

The other rig often used in surf fishing is the "fish-finder" rig. The fish-finder has a ring on one end and a snap on the other. The sinker is held by the snap while the line runs through the ring. A leather thong and barrel swivel is tied to the end of the line after it is run through the ring, then a leader is attached to the barrel swivel with the hook. The idea here is to allow a suspicious fish to pick up the bait and move off without dragging the sinker. The line just slides freely through the ring of the fish finger gadget. When you cast or retrieve the rig, the leather thong acts as a stop.

Both these rigs are used with pyramid sinkers if the bottom is sandy. However, over rocky bottoms, round or bank sinkers are better. If the crabs are bothering the bait or you want the bait to float off the bottom, you can add a cork float to the leader just above the hook. These come in various sizes and can be bought in almost any tackle store. Both these rigs can be used with spinning or conventional tackle. With spinning tackle, though, you use smaller hooks, sinkers, and swivels; with conventional tackle you use the larger ones.

There are variations of the rigs above which are used for flounders, blackfish or tautog, and other fish caught in the surf. These are specifically designed for a particular fish and should be used when called for.

Chapter 6

Wind, Weather, Water, and Tides

It takes much more to be a successful surf angler than just having the proper tackle, lures, and baits. A good surf angler is also a keen observer and student of winds, weather, water, tides, and the food present in the surf. All of these may affect the fishing either by being beneficial or detrimental.

Take winds, for example, and their effect on surf fishing. They have ruined more trips than any other lone factor, yet winds also have been responsible for some of the best surf fishing. Although this may sound contradictory, it all depends on the velocity and direction of the wind, time of year, and, of course, the type of waves encountered.

Generally speaking, along the Atlantic Coast winds from the east, northeast, south, southeast and southwest when fairly strong create waves and moderate-to-heavy surf. North, northwest, and west winds, on the other hand, flatten the surf.

During the late spring and summer months the prevailing winds are from the south and southwest. A wind from the south if light doesn't affect the fishing too much. If it is strong, then it makes casting difficult; if it blows for any length of time, it dirties the water with debris and seaweed, making fishing generally poor.

A southwest wind if light or moderate often provides good fishing. It brings warm water and is usually strong enough to create white water along the surf, on sand or rock bars, and around rocky points. It washes out a variety of food and scatters schools of baitfish. The first day or two of a southwest wind are usually most productive. If it blows for several days or increases in strength, the fishing often slows down or stops. When strong, a southwest wind makes it difficult to cast and work a lure. However, when some kind of baitfish, such as mullet, are present in the surf the fishing is often excellent despite the strong southwest wind. At such times the baitfish may be at your feet or a short distance out and can be reached with short casts.

When the wind blows out of the southeast, east, or northeast, the fishing may be good for the first day or two. As the wind increases or keeps on blowing, the waves get big and ground swells may result. At such times you may find good fishing along certain rocky shores, mussel or rock bars, and in protected coves. Along sandy shores the water will usually be roiled and dirty with suspended particles of sand, causing the fishing to be poor. If the storm continues, the wind and big waves may make fishing almost impossible or hazardous.

After a storm, the wind either dies or shifts to the west, northwest, or north. This is the time you should head for the surf, for some of the best fishing takes place when the ocean settles down a bit. The fish are hungry, the baitfish are on the move again, and various crabs, clams, worms, and other marine creatures have been washed out of their hiding places.

If the wind blows strong for any length of time from the west, northwest, or north, it will calm the ocean and clean the water. Then the fishing often slows down or stops completely. This is usually the case in the spring, but in the late fall, as the water gets colder, the fish feed more heavily on baitfish. The lower temperature of the water makes the gamefish hungrier and more active. At such times, the fish will often feed despite the fact that the wind has flattened the water and made it clear. West, northwest, and north winds are offshore winds along the Atlantic Coast and tend to make the baitfish hug the shoreline in compact schools. This in turn attracts the larger gamefish which often come in very close to the beaches at such times.

Such expressions as "white water," "bass water," "perfect conditions," "dirty water," and similar talk among surf fishermen are used often to describe the condition of the water. The terms "white water" and "bass water" are used when the surf is fairly rough and there are plenty of waves breaking to create foamy, white water on the sand, rock, or mussel bars. Striped bass fishing is usually better when there is plenty of white water since they feed more actively at such times and strike lures more readily.

When there are "perfect conditions" it means that there is enough white water, the tide is right for the locality, and there are baitfish present. At such times, fishing should be and often is good since conditions are attractive to the fish, particularly the striped bass. However, there are always exceptions in surf fishing, and many a time conditions seem perfect yet the fish aren't there or aren't biting. Still the odds are more in your favor when fishing under perfect conditions than when one or more of the necessary factors—white water, bait, tide, and so on—are missing.

"Dirty water" can ruin the surf fishing for two or three days or even longer. When the water is dirty, it means that there is debris, seaweed, or suspended sand particles which make it impossible to fish. The debris or seaweed fouls the line or the lure on almost every cast. Rarely are fish present or do they strike under such conditions. If the water is a dirty brown from suspended sand this also stops the fishing. Slightly dirty water of a very light brown or milky green color may even create good fishing. Some of the best striped bass fishing I ever had occurred when the water was slightly discolored. The fish do not get a chance to examine the lure or see the leader or line at such times and strike with less hesitation. They also seem hungrier because the water during the preceding days was too dirty for them to feed. So when it starts to clear they strike with a vengeance.

Then we have "calm water" conditions where the water is crystal clear. As mentioned earlier in this section, such a condition usually results from an offshore wind or no wind for a few days. Generally speaking, "calm water" means poor fishing except late in the fall of the year, on certain nights, or when the baitfish are unusually thick. Such fish as striped bass seem to know that it is more difficult to catch baitfish when the water is clear, so they wait until the water gets rough or at night when conditions are more favorable. Even if they do feed, they are harder to fool in calm water since they can see the lure, leader, and line.

Tides also play an important part in surf fishing. The question of which tide is best for fishing depends on the area being fished. As a rule, if you use artificial lures you'll find that some of the best fishing will take place at the low tides. The last of the outgoing tide and the start of the incoming tide are especially favored. However, the start of the outgoing tide at high water also produces good fishing at times in many areas. My experience has been that slack water is a poor time for surf fishing.

One reason why the low tides or half-tides are better for fishing is because there is more white water at such times. Another reason is that the baitfish are more concentrated in smaller areas. At high tide most of the sand bars, mussel bars, and rocks will be covered by plenty of water. The waves coming in rarely break and create white water, but when the tide is about half out and during low water, the rocks, bars, and reefs are exposed or covered by shallow water. Then when a wave comes rolling in it breaks and creates plenty of white water. So at high tide, even if baitfish are present, most surf fish don't bother them. Later, when it drops they commence to feed.

However, in some places, such as deep holes with outer sand bars, coves, and similar spots where fish can get trapped, they often wait until high tide before moving in to feed. During the low tides such places are too shallow and the big fish stay out. But when the tide gets high they move in to feed on the baitfish or sea life which is usually present in such spots.

Another good general rule is to fish with artificial lures at the low and half-tides and with natural bait during the high tides. Baitfish are easier to catch, more concentrated during low water, and at high tide tend to scatter, making them harder to catch. Surf fish often feed on the bottom on crabs, clams, seaworms, and similar foods.

In fact, food plays a big part in any kind of surf fishing. The presence of food in the surf will bring in fish quicker than any other single factor. Most surf fishermen are always on the lookout for baitfish because they know that sooner or later they will attract the larger gamefish. An indication of how important such baitfish can be is shown in the following incident. I was fishing a certain beach late one afternoon with a metal squid. While coming off a wood jetty which I had fished without a strike, I noticed a school of mullet in the wash, almost on the beach. I watched as the small fish would hurry back into deeper water as the wave receded. Then on the next wave they would come back again. For a minute or two I observed them in that one area just moving back and forth with the waves. Then I continued on down the beach fishing as I went. I had no luck and now the sun was nearing the horizon. Remembering the school of mullet, I started back to the spot. When I arrived at the jetty I saw the baitfish leaping for their lives as a school of striped bass chased them. On the very first cast, I hooked a fish and before it was all over, there were seven stripers lying on the sand.

Towards evening, baitfish usually move close inshore to seek the protection of the shallow water. The larger gamefish often follow and good fishing occurs at dusk and at night. During the day, you have to watch for leaping baitfish, gamefish, or gulls and terns wheeling and diving.

Too much bait can be as bad as no bait. The fish often feed so much that either they aren't interested in your lures or do not chase a single lure or baitfish, but instead wait until a large, compact school of bait comes by. At such times your best bet is to cast right into the school of baitfish when you see a gamefish swirl or break water.

Many surf fishermen also study the phases of the moon carefully since they are certain it affects the fishing. It has been my experience that the moon does affect surf fishing to a considerable extent. Year in and year out you'll find that some of the best fishing will take place around the new moon and full moon periods. At such times the tides and rips are strongest, the tides are higher, and surf fish find it easier to catch the more helpless baitfish. Also at these periods the water is rougher and ground swells more common. If the water is not dirty, which is often the case, then the surf fishing is apt to be good.

When the moon is full you will often have good fishing at night. The strong light makes it easier for gamefish to see the lures and find the baitfish. This is especially true during the fall of the year when such baitfish as mullet, menhaden, herring, and shiners are migrating along the coast. They often move on moonlit nights, and striped bass, bluefish, weakfish, and other gamefish come in to feed on them.

Baitfish and gamefish are somewhat less active on dark nights, but there is often good fishing to be had. Surf fish can see a lure on the darkest night and many a fine catch is made then. About the only condition which makes for poor fishing at night is when there is a lot of phosphorescence present. This lights up your lure and leaves a trail which makes fish suspicious. And the two extremes—calm, flat water and very rough water—also result in poor fishing at night as well as in the day. The two best times to go surf fishing is from about an hour before daybreak until the sun gets too high, and then again, at sundown about an hour before dark until two or three hours after dark. If you fish these two periods year in and year out, you'll catch more fish in the surf than during the middle of the day or night.

The weather itself affects fishing mostly through the winds prevailing during the given day, as explained earlier. But if the day is sunny and hot, fish at daybreak, dusk, or at night as a general rule. About the only exceptions are in the early spring and late fall when the water is cold: then fish are often caught in the middle of the day. Also, when the day is cloudy or stormy good fishing may occur during the middle of the day. Of course, we're talking mainly of fishing for gamefish, such as striped bass, bluefish, weakfish, and channel bass, which chase baitfish. Other fish, such as northern or southern whiting (kingfish), tautog or blackfish, and croakers, which feed on the bottom, can be caught all day long at times.

One of the main reasons why many surf fishermen do not catch striped bass is because they fish when they feel like it and not when the fish are feeding. I've had such men come to me and say, "I've been at this surf fishing for 10 years and I've yet to catch my first striped bass." Or they complain because they never caught a big striper. When I asked them when they go surf fishing, they almost invariably tell me that they get down to the beach when the sun is already up, usually around 7 or 8 o'clock in the morning, fish throughout the middle of the day, and quit around 3 or 4 o'clock in the afternoon. No wonder they don't catch striped bass—they're fishing too late in the morning and quitting too early in the afternoon or evening.

Chapter 7

Fishing Sand Beaches

Most surf fishing is done from sand beaches which front our long coastlines along the Atlantic, Gulf, and Pacific coasts. Here the problem of locating fish in the surf is one which confronts both the novice and expert surf angler. Before you can catch any fish in the surf you must know where to fish. These days this is often solved for the surf angler with little or no effort on his part. For example, when there is a run of fish in a certain spot which attracts surf anglers the local rod and gun club or outdoors writer of a newspaper sooner or later mentions this hot fishing. And surf anglers head for the spot.

Then again, with more and more anglers fishing the surf, it is not unusual for one of them to locate fish and spread the word to fishing tackle dealers and friends. Soon you'll find surf anglers lined up along the beach all casting with some chance of taking fish. Here the surf angler just arriving at the beach joins the line and can thank the earlier anglers for putting him on the fish.

Suppose, though, you don't read about a run of fish or don't see other anglers fishing. How do you go about locating fish along a sand beach? Well, the obvious way is to look for diving or wheeling gulls or terns. When there are birds actively feeding on small baitfish, it's a good sign that the larger gamefish are under them. Of course, such activity by birds is only reliable when there are schools of baitfish around. If the fish are feeding deep on some other kind of marine life, you won't see the birds. In order to cover as much territory as possible, surf anglers drive along roads parallel to the beach watching for signs of bird activity or other anglers catching fish. Where the hard roads end or the going is tough, special beach buggies equipped with oversize tires and other refinements are used to drive on the soft sand.

One point to remember about birds is that when they are sitting on the water, keep an eye on them. They may be merely resting and waiting for the gamefish to drive the baitfish to the surface again. If the birds are working quite some distance from shore, keep watching them. Often the baitfish and school of fish will move in closer so that you can reach them. Or wait until dusk when the baitfish move in to shore.

If there are no signs of birds working, study the water carefully to see if there are any baitfish present. If the baitfish are there and you see them skip or leap out of the water, start casting with surface plugs or metal squids. On many occasions you can see the larger gamefish themselves leaping out of the water or swirling as they pursue the smaller baitfish.

One advantage possessed by a veteran surf angler which the novice lacks is ability to "read" the water along sand beaches as a clue to fishing spots. Unless you possess this knowledge you will waste many precious hours casting and fishing in unproductive waters. (The discouraging thing about the matter is that it often takes a long time to learn how to read the water.)

How, then, can a beginner fish a sandy beach with any chance of success? Well, it was mentioned previously that you could discover a fishing spot by watching other anglers. If there is no one on the beach to guide you, there is one method which can often be used although it means plenty of casting and walking. When using this system you make two or three casts at regular intervals and within areas of about 50 ft. apart. In other words, you cast two or three times in one spot. Then you move down the beach about 50 ft. and make two or three more casts and so on down the line. On many occasions I've covered two or three miles of beach using this method, and often I would work my way back, too. Here you can use one type of lure, such as a metal squid, on the way down and on the way back change to a plug or a rigged eel.

If you want to cover the maximum area using this method, you don't cast straight out into the ocean when you stop. Instead you make one cast to your left at an angle, the next one straight in front of you, and the third to your right. This way your lure travels over different water each time.

Of course, if you get a hit or hook a fish, you should stop and fish that spot for several minutes before moving on. After locating a fishy looking area, you can work it more carefully.

This method can be used when two anglers are fishing together. Both anglers start about 50 ft. apart, then one passes up the other. After a few minutes the second angler passes up the first and so on down the line. If you decide to separate, some sort of signaling system should be worked out so that if one angler hits into fish or locates a school he can call the other one. At night a loud whistle or blinking lights can be used. In the daytime you can wave your arms or rod to call your buddy.

However, instead of casting haphazardly along a sandy beach, you can save time and energy by concentrating on likely spots. There are many signs and clues which show the type of bottom, depth of water, currents, food, and fish which may be found in a given spot. The color of the water is a good indication of depth. Dark blue, dark green, or green water shows that there is plenty of water and indicates a hole, slough, or channel. These usually harbor food and fish. Light green or yellowish water shows shallow spots when the water is calm. When the water is rough these shallow spots have foamy white water or brownish water if the sand is stirred up. There are good spots for stripers.

The action of the waves also provides a clue. Waves breaking some distance from the beach indicate a sand bar; on a gently sloping beach where they first curl and break indicate a drop-off and is a good spot to cast to. In fact, it's always a good idea to cast your lure about 20 to 30 ft. beyond the first line of breakers and reel it through the wash.

When big waves do not break until they reach shore, the beach usually slopes sharply with deep water close to shore. Here you can often catch big striped bass, bluefish, weakfish, channel bass, and other surf fish on a short cast.

If you notice the waves curl and break to create white water then stop foaming to pass quietly over a darker spot, it means that there's a hole, pocket, or slough inside the outer sand bar. These are favorite hangouts of striped bass, channel bass, weakfish, and other fish which lie in wait for baitfish or other food the waves wash out. The outer

Modern surf anglers like this Massachusetts fellow depend on beach buggies to take them through the soft sand to distant spots.

bar running parallel to the beach usually has a slough on the inside. One of the best spots for striped bass is where the sand bar drops off into this slough or hole. The crashing waves wash food right into the striper's mouth. Here you should cast your lure on the sand bar and reel it into the slough.

Sand bars never run without a break. Every so often there are cuts or channels through which the water enters and leaves. Fishing for most surf fish is good at these places. The cuts or channels are often deep, the curent is strong, and a rip is created outside. Crabs, sand bugs, clams, and baitfish are more helpless in these waters, which make easy pickings for the big fish.

When the tide drops and gets near low, there may not be enough water on the sand bars and in the sloughs for good fishing. At such times, it is often possible to wade out through the slough and up on the sand bar to fish the outside edge. Here a good cast will put your lure or bait out in deep water again and get you some fish.

One good general rule is to fish beaches with sand bars when the water is rough. Then the waves break on the bars and lose some of

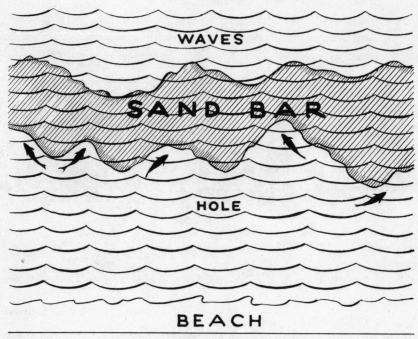

WAVES

SAND BAR

HOLE

BEACH

FISH LYING INSIDE SAND BAR

their force besides creating plenty of white water. On the other hand, when the water is calm look for a sharply sloping beach where there is deep water right near shore.

Inlets or rivers entering into the ocean along sandy beaches are always good surf fishing spots. This is especially so in the spring and fall of the year when baitfish enter or leave such inlets or rivers. Surf fish are usually waiting for them on an outgoing tide, and you can have good fishing if you are there at the right time.

How you work your lures along a sandy beach may mean the difference between fish and no fish. When using metal squids—or any lure, in fact—try to cast behind a breaking wave. Otherwise, an incoming wave will pick up your lure and bring it in faster than you can take up the slack. A slack line will stop the action of your lure and cause it to sink. Even if you do get a strike you won't be able to hook the fish.

However, when a wave breaks and rushes back to sea it creates an undertow and terrific resistance against your squid. Now you have to slow down your reeling, otherwise your lure will spin or revolve.

Generally, a slow or medium retrieve is best with a metal squid along sandy beaches, but for bluefish, bonito, albacore, or other fast moving species a fast retrieve is called for. When the water is calm and clear, fast reeling usually fools the fish more readily than when it is rough. Try different speeds until you find the one which the fish want.

You should also try different depths when fishing metal squids. Of course, if the fish are on top, you should hold your rod tip high and reel fairly fast to keep it moving near the surface. If the fish aren't showing, try slower reeling to get down deeper with the metal squid. Sometimes, should you let your metal squid sink to the bottom then start a slow reel, you may get one of those lazy fish lying down deep. Bucktail or feather jigs are especially effective when worked in this manner.

When using surface plugs along a sandy beach, keep them moving fairly fast at all times and cause plenty of commotion on top of the water. If there are any mullet or baitfish moving along in the water, cast your surface plug a few feet beyond them and reel through them. Underwater plugs should be reeled more slowly and you should feel them working at all times. When a wave comes in reel a bit fast; when it recedes, slow down.

Sand beaches lend themselves well to bottom fishing with natural baits. Except for baitfish swimming on top or near the surface, most of the food is found down near the bottom. So a crab, seaworm, piece of clam, squid, or fish cast into a likely looking cut, slough, or hole will often produce when artificial lures fail. The best procedure when baitfishing is to make a long cast, then let the lure lie on the bottom in one spot for a few minutes. Then you reel in a few feet slowly and let it lie in a new spot. Continue doing this until your lure is at your feet. If you get poor results after several casts, move down the beach and try another spot.

Landing a hooked fish along a sandy beach presents less of a problem than in other areas, such as rocky beaches or jetties. If you hook a fish here you can let him run freely. Usually the fish will head out to sea or run parallel to the beach. If he moves off to the left or right too sharply the angler is forced to follow and keep reeling until he's opposite the fish again. On many occasions, when fishing popular spots with other anglers to your left and right, you have to shout to let them know you have a fish on so that they can reel their lines in.

The important thing to remember is not to strain the rod or line to the breaking point. Always keep your rod tip as high as you can and lower it only for a second or two when the fish leaps or rushes unexpectedly. Then quickly raise it again.

The crucial period in fighting a fish arises when the fish is almost licked and is near the beach. The waves are strong here and the undertow or backwash also pulls on the fish. When the seas are rough it may be a real job to bring a fish, especially a big one, past the waves. You have to watch the waves carefully. When a wave breaks and sweeps in you have to reel fast to gain line and take up the slack. When a wave recedes you let the fish go out again, or if the strain isn't too great you hold him in one spot. It will take longer to land a fish with a spinning outfit than with a conventional rod and reel.

You may also need a gaff when using a spinning outfit to beach a fish more quickly. With a conventional outfit you can usually wait until a big wave washes a fish in and lands him high and dry on the sand.

The angler who fishes sandy beaches must continually explore and study the shoreline. Sandy beaches are always changing due to shifting sands, erosion, storms, and currents. A section of beach which may be good this season may be poor next year. Or a section which was poor last season may be a hot spot this year. That sand bar which produced so many fish last fall may disappear next spring. So it pays to go down to the beach each spring and as often as possible to study the shoreline to see if any major changes have taken place.

Chapter 8

Fishing Rocky Shores

Although most surf fishing is done along sandy beaches, there is also some excellent fishing along rocky shores. Such rocky shores are found mostly along the East Coast in Maine, Massachusetts, Rhode Island, Montauk Point, New York, and on the West Coast in Washington, Oregon, and parts of California. A variety of surf fish can be caught along rocky shores, but on the East Coast the striped bass and blackfish or tautog are the two species usually taken. On the West Coast there are many kinds of rockfishes, surf perches, and greenling which are taken in rocky areas.

Rocky shores have several advantages over sandy beaches. First, they attract marine life, such as shellfish, crabs, and small fish, which in turn attract the larger fish. Second, they enable the surf angler to fish high and dry in many spots and yet reach deep water with short casts. Last but not least, rocky shores seldom change much and good fishing spots produce year after year. In fact, any veteran surf angler familiar with a rocky shoreline, such as Rhode Island, can show you a boulder, sunken rock, or small cove where thousands of striped bass have been taken in past years.

Naturally it takes quite a bit of fishing to locate such spots. Usually the surf angler tries a few casts in likely looking spots along rocky shores. If he catches a fish there or gets some strikes, he makes a mental note of the spot and tries again at some future date. After he fishes such a spot under varying tides and weather conditions, he gets a pretty good idea of the best time to fish such spots.

A beginner fishing a rocky shore, however, is at a disadvantage because he doesn't have this knowledge or background to help him. If he uses the trial-and-error method, it may take him years to find all the good spots. Fortunately, rocky shores have certain similarities which can serve as a guide to locating good fishing spots even in a strange area.

63

Along rocky shores you'll often find high cliffs which border deep
water. To a beginner these look like perfect fishing spots, but they are
usually avoided by the veteran surf angler, mainly because he will
sometimes have to fish from a point perhaps 30 or 40 ft. above the
water. This is too high to work artificial lures effectively, and a fish
has to be lifted too far to land him. With small species this may be
practical, but if you hook a big fish you will usually lose him. Most
surf anglers look for low rocks where they can stand a few feet above
the water.

Some of these high rocks have sloping sides, or they slope toward
the water and can be fished at these sections. There is often a ledge
along the front. The breaking waves crash against this ledge creating
a fringe of white water. Stripers rarely strike the lure in the deeper,
clearer water some distance from shore in such spots. Instead, they
may be cruising in this deep water but dash into the white water
close to the rocks to grab a baitfish. In most cases, the lure is cast a
short distance out and then reeled through the white water. I have
watched schools of small stripers following a metal squid or underwater plug in the deeper water, then as it was about to disappear in
the white water, one of them would sometimes grab it. The best tech-

*Anglers fishing rocky shores often like to climb up on a high rock for easier casting and control
of the line and fish.*

nique here is to reel pretty fast in the deeper, clearer water, then as the lure reaches the white water, slow it down as if it were a weak or crippled baitfish.

If there are any sharp breaks in the high cliffs and boulders forming small coves or gullies, study such spots carefully. Here, if the water is deep enough to harbor a striper or other fish. you will often find good fishing. The waves sweep in and then recede, creating a backwash which makes a favorite hangout for striped bass. Your lure should be cast and reeled through such a gully along both sides.

The high cliffs or rocks with deep water nearby are good spots to fish for bluefish, weakfish, mackerel, bonito, albacore, and other fish which do not particularly like the shallow, white water. They often can be seen feeding on schools of baitfish migrating along the coast in the spring and fall months.

The high rocks are also favorite bottom fishing spots with natural baits. Rocky shores are difficult to fish with sinkers since too many rigs are fouled and lost. Especially bad is casting into shallow water from the water level because the sinker quickly catches behind some

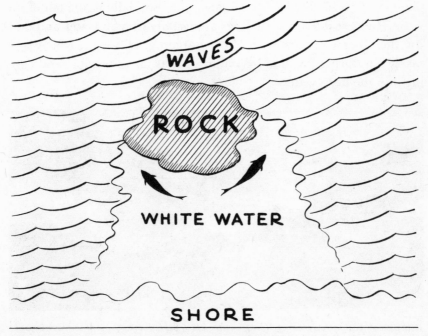

LOCATION OF FISH BEHIND ROCK

rocks or kelp. From the high rocks, though, you can often drop your sinker and bait into some deep hole almost straight down or at a slight angle and not get tangled so often.

Usually close to the high cliffs and rocks you will find lower ones, such as rocky points, which jut out into deeper water. These are good spots to fish since the waves crashing against the point create white water. You can cover quite a bit of territory in an arc to your left and right when fishing from such a rocky point.

One of the most difficult spots to fish along rocky shores are the places where there are rocks, boulders, and stones of varied sizes scattered in profusion over a broad area. The reason why they are tough is because any sinking or underwater lure, such as metal squids, underwater plugs, or rigged eels, are easily hung up and lost in those spots. However, the profusion of rocks makes for good fishing on many occasions. Such places are especially good after a storm when the ground swells come sweeping in to turn the whole place a foaming white. Stripers love these conditions and come in to feed. A metal squid reeled fast through this water brings a hard strike. Surface plugs are also good in such a shallow spot, especially in the fall of the year. The best tides in such areas are usually at high water and during the first two hours or so of the outgoing. However, I have also taken fish during low tide by wading out as far as possible and casting into the deep water.

Rocky shores such as this one at Narragansett, Rhode Island, offer some of the best striped bass fishing.

Coves, both big and small, also produce fish along rocky shores. In fact, it is in such spots that some of the largest, as well as many of the smaller, fish are taken. The formations of the coves vary in that some may have exposed rocks and boulders while others seem rock free with more open water. This is often deceiving because most of the coves have some kind of rocks underwater, covered with kelp and seaweed, that provide many holes and pockets where fish, particularly striped bass, like to lie and feed.

You can catch fish in coves during the daytime, especially when the water is rough. What makes them good spots to fish during a storm, if there is a rocky barrier which breaks the waves, is that the smaller baitfish take shelter in the coves and big fish come in to feed on them. However, coves are also very productive at night. Some of them have deep water even at low tide, and they can be fished then. But, as a general rule, the coves have shallow water and are best around the high tides.

It may take quite a bit of time to locate the submerged rocks and boulders in a cove. You can go out in a boat to get a good idea of their location if the water is calm or clear, or you can try spotting them from a high cliff if there is one nearby. Most anglers find such rocks and boulders by casting. When their lure hangs up or touches the rock, they know the location and reel it a bit faster next time. The holes where stripers or other fish lie are located by catching a fish or getting a strike. After getting a few such strikes or catching fish, you know where to cast the next time. In fishing such coves it is always a good idea to regard every bump or touch as a strike. Many of these will not be, but if you come back with rod tip you will hook fish that otherwise would be missed.

Those coves which have exposed boulders, rocks, or reefs are easy to fish. The striped bass will almost invariably lie just inside the rocks on the shore side where the water is a foamy white. Generally, it takes only one or two casts to discover if a fish is present. After you catch a bass from such a hide, you can often come back in a few hours or next day or in a few days and take another fish or two. Stripers do not let such favored feeding stations stay empty for long. New fish are always moving in after the old ones leave or are caught.

If you ever locate a school of stripers in one of these coves, you may experience some fast fishing. Most of the time they will be the smaller school fish, but sometimes big stripers up to 50 lbs. may be present. However, these big fish are usually "loners," and if you get one or two big ones from a cove you're doing well.

One type of rocky shore which provides good fishing is the rock or mussel bar, wherein one finds the smaller round rocks or growths of mussels which extend far out with deep water or holes in front or on the sides. (Matunuck Beach in Rhode Island and the North Bar at Montauk, Long Island, are representative of this kind of shore.) The fisherman has to wade out in the water up to his hips and cast out in front of the bar or in any hole on the left or right. These rock or mussel bars are usually good when the water is rough and baitfish take refuge in the shallows. Metal squids, jigs, and surface plugs are the best lures to use here. Any sinking lure used must be reeled fast or it will get hung up. To hold the fish, one also needs a long stringer since he may be out in the water more than 200 ft. from shore.

Inlets entering into the ocean are also excellent along rocky shores. Here the rip on an outgoing tide sweeps baitfish, crabs, and other foods to the waiting fish.

When fishing rocky shores certain precautions must be taken for safety. Always wear a pair of wading sandals or ice-creepers over your boots or waders when fishing rocky shores. The lower rocks are usually covered with seaweed, moss, or slime so a slip can be dangerous. Avoid walking on the mossy, wet rocks which slope into the water. For better footing, pick the level rocks covered with mussels or barnacles.

After you hook the fish, start working your way down to these rocks early in the fight. Then when the fish is licked you can maneuver him into the landing area and wait until a helping wave sweeps him up high and dry. In some spots you can work the fish between two rocks or into a shallow pool, then go down and pick him up. A gaff is usually not required along such rocky shores unless you happen to wade out into the water. Grabbing an active fish with your hands can be dangerous, especially if he has a plug in his mouth.

Rocky shores are somewhat difficult to fish since you often have to do quite a bit of walking and climbing over rocks. Don't let anybody tell you that isn't tough work, especially with a heavy pair of waders and on a hot day or night, but I'd rather fish the surf along rocky shores than almost anywhere else. Each rocky point, cove, or bar presents an individual problem, which must be solved, of where to cast, how to work the lure, and how to land the fish. This challenge makes for interesting fishing, and I for one never get bored when surf fishing along rocky shores. If I get tired of fishing one spot, I can either move on to the next one to see what it has to offer or can hop into the car and drive to another rocky area.

Chapter 9

Fishing Jetties and Breakwaters

In order to build cities, towns, resorts, and beaches for bathing, man has leveled many of the sand dunes which acted as Nature's fortresses against the advancing sea. The result is that many homes, boardwalks, roads, and other structures are threatened with destruction or flooding. Sand beaches are continually shrinking in size as the sand is washed out to sea, and inlets and channels used by boats are always being filled in or changed. To combat these forces of the sea and prevent beach erosion many jetties and breakwaters have been built along our coasts. These safeguards are especially numerous in Long Island and along the New Jersey coast, but almost every inlet and harbor is now protected by long breakwaters.

Jetties and breakwaters often provide good surf fishing spots, especially for fish which normally hesitate to venture close to shore. Almost every salt-water fish found in a given area can be caught from a jetty or breakwater at one time or another. Many of the better jetties have produced record-sized surf fish, such as striped bass, bluefish, weakfish, and other gamefish. As for the bottom species, such as tautog or blackfish, flounders, snappers, groupers, and similar fish, a jetty or breakwater is one of the best spots to fish.

Let's look at the bigger breakwaters and long jetties first to see how they can be fished effectively. These are the long, broad, rock or concrete structures usually built at the entrances to inlets or harbors to keep the channels clear for ships or boats. Some of them may run out to sea for two miles or more. In some places, notably the Gulf of Mexico, these breakwaters and jetties are often topped with concrete, making them flat and easy to walk on. Those constructed from boulders or rocks are also flat when new, but as the years go by the rocks fall apart and walking on them becomes more difficult. However, since most breakwaters and long jetties are high, the rocks usually remain dry and do not become moss covered, except near the water line. All in all, they are comparatively safe and comfortable fishing platforms.

As a general rule, the long breakwaters and jetties found near inlets have the surf or ocean on one side and the inlet or bay on the other. Where the breakwater just begins on the ocean side, you'll find some surf, which is a good spot to fish for striped bass. During the fall of the year when mullets are in big schools you will often find good fishing in such spots since stripers, channel bass, bluefish, weakfish, and other fish drive the small baitfish into the corner formed by the breakwater and the beach. This spot is usually best when the water is fairly rough.

Moving along the breakwater you will sometimes take striped bass near the rocks in the deeper water, especially when waves breaking against them turn the water a foamy white alongside the structure. However, as you move out on the breakwater and fish the deeper water, you'll find such fish as bluefish, pollock, weakfish, and mackerel in northern waters and tarpon, sea trout, snook, jack crevalle, and Spanish mackerel in the South. If you fish on the bottom with bait or use live baitfish, you can catch the bottom feeders, such as northern and southern whiting (kingfish), croakers, flounders, blackfish or tautog, sheepshead, pompano and jewfish, snappers, and groupers.

These species and others are often taken on both sides of a breakwater or jetty. Surf anglers fishing these structures with artificial lures, such as rigged eels, plugs, metal squids, or spoons, usually wait until the fish show on the surface or until someone catches the first fish. But you can also fish blind by working along the breakwater and stopping to cast at intervals of around 50 ft. In that way you can cover the entire structure out to the end. There is usually a good current or tide alongside the breakwater, although one of the hot spots is the end of the breakwater or jetty. Here the tides clash, creating a rip which traps baitfish and attracts the larger gamefish.

When the gamefish are chasing the baitfish on or near the surface, top-water plugs often work well. If you use metal squids or spoons, reel them fairly fast to keep them riding high. However, when the fish aren't showing, you can often get them with underwater plugs or by letting the metal squids, spoons, and jigs sink deep and then by reeling them back slowly and erratically.

Fishing the shallow waters near shore on the breakwaters and long jetties is best at dusk, during the night, and at daybreak. Later on, as the sun gets high, the fish move into deeper water and fishing can be done near the end of the structures.

The smaller rock jetties which may be anywhere from a hundred feet to several hundred feet long are more numerous than the breakwaters. They often are found for many miles at regular intervals, usually about a city block. When first put in and new they are also broad and high, making for easy walking. But they are generally lower and narrower than the breakwaters and soon become covered with slimy moss. In a few years storms break up the jetties and the rocks fall apart. These older jetties are tougher to fish and are more dangerous, but they all produce fish at one time or another.

Rock jetties change somewhat each year because shifting sands may fill in one side and currents may wash out holes on the other. Sand bars are often found in front of the jetties. So a close watch is necessary to find out which jetties are most productive during a given year or season. Generally, however, if there is fairly deep water around the jetty on either side or in front, then there is a good chance of taking fish. The higher, newer jetties can be fished at the high tides when the water isn't too rough, but the lower, older jetties are often covered at high tide and call for fishing at low tide. On some of these jetties you can get out part way when the tide is half out to fish the sides. When the tide is near low, the end is usually the best spot.

Most of the jetties have a fairly strong current at the end and along the sides. Striped bass like to lie or prowl around such jetties. When the tide is high and you can get out part way on a jetty, you can cast from the sides. To cover the water you can cast in a semi-circle—first toward the end of the jetty, then a bit farther away, and so on—until your lure has covered most of the water. After doing this a few times with the same or different lures, you can go over to the other side of the jetty and cover that water. You'll find that many of your strikes from striped bass will come when your lure is near the jetty. Stripers like to follow a lure in, then hit it when it is caught in the wash and rip created alongside the rocks. For this reason it always pays to make a few casts alongside the jetty so that your lure swims close to the rocks, following a course like the baitfish do.

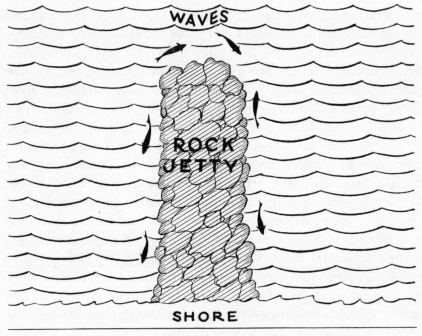

LOCATION OF FISH AROUND JETTY

If the jetty is high, or the tide is low, then you can usually go out to the very end. This is the best spot for striped bass, bluefish, weakfish, and other surf fish because the water is deeper and the currents and rips are strongest. Baitfish, such as mullet, like to hug the shoreline, but jetties act as barriers and force them to swim around the end. The larger fish are often waiting for them when they come around the front of the jetty. The best way to fish the end of the jetty is to "fan" it in a semicircle, making a cast first to your left, then slightly more to the right, the next one still farther to the right, and so on until you cover all the water in front of you. Some of your fish will be hooked way out, but stripers will often take the lure a short distance out in front of the jetty. It is important to keep your lure working right up to the rocks.

If the rock jetties are long or in bad condition, it is tough work to fish more than one or two of them. However, if the jetties are short and fairly flat, then you can often cover several jetties in one tide or during a night. The night time is usually the best time to fish jetties since they are generally found in well-populated areas where bathers

crowd the beaches during the daytime. Naturally, this is mostly true
during the summer months. Later on in the fall when the weather
turns cool, you can often fish during the day. However, when fishing
for stripers off jetties the best fishing, like anywhere else, usually takes
place at daybreak, dusk, or during the night. One bad feature about
fishing jetties is that on weekends and holidays they are often taken
by other anglers. To fish the end of a rock jetty properly there should
be no more than one or two anglers casting there. I warn of this not
only because of interference, and decreased chances of taking fish,
but also for safety's sake. Yet surf anglers often try to crowd the end
of a small jetty, a condition that makes casting dangerous and the
chances of taking fish reduced. Besides, one of the main appeals of
surf fishing—at least to me—is to have plenty of elbow room to fish
relaxed in comfort and to have plenty of water to try different lures,
techniques, and so on without interference. This is not possible when
fishing next to other anglers on a jetty. Because this is more like pier
fishing or boat fishing than surf fishing, most veteran anglers shy away
from crowded jetties to look for empty ones.

Wooden jetties, which are also found along sand beaches, are the
narrow catwalks that run out from 50 to 200 or 300 ft. They
have piles for supports on both sides and long piles on the end or
head of the wooden jetty. Very few, if any, of these jetties can be
fished at high tide since the water covers them. But when the tide is

Some of the popular breakwaters and jetties get crowded on weekends. This is Manasquan,
New Jersey.

from half out to half in it is often possible to go out near the end for good fishing. Here striped bass also like to lie alongside the wood jetties waiting for baitfish or crabs to come by.

In fact, it is often possible from wood jetties to hook stripers almost at your feet. Many a time I've had a fish follow my lure in alongside the jetty, then grab it a rod length or so away. For this reason, one of the most effective ways to fish wood jetties is to cast out toward the end and work the lure alongside as close as possible. This can be done several times on both sides, although the best fishing is found usually on the deeper side.

If you can get out to the end of the wood jetty, you'll often take bigger fish. In the strong current at the end of the jetty, as well as on the inside edge of any sand bar, the fish lie in and feed within casting distance. Here, too, white water breaking on the bars and strong currents alongside of the jetty make for the best fishing.

Wood jetties can be dangerous places to fish if the water is rough. Even when it is calm, a wood jetty is slippery and should never be fished without wearing ice-creepers. These dig into the hard, moss-covered wood—slick as ice when damp or wet—to provide firm footing. Of course, at low tide when you get out toward the end of the wood jetty, you'll find it covered with mussels and here you don't have to worry so much about slipping.

Landing a hooked fish on a wood jetty can be tricky until you get

Wood jetties like this one often produce good fishing along the New York and New Jersey coasts.

used to the procedure. When you do hook a fish, stay in place until the fish completes his first run or two, then start backing up toward the beach slowly while holding your rod tip high and fighting the fish. Actually, you walk slowly sideways facing the water on the side the fish is hooked. If the fish tries to run around the end of the jetty he should be stopped or turned at all costs. Otherwise your line will foul around the piles or get cut on the mussels. Once you have the fish well inside the end of the jetty or away from it, you can keep moving off the structure. When you reach the area where the waves break, you back up still more nearer to shore, then wait. When a wave comes in, reel fast as it sweeps the fish toward the beach. When the wave recedes, hold the fish in one spot or let him go again if the strain on the rod and line is too great. You may have to do this back and forth several times before a big wave finally deposits the fish high and dry on the sand where you can jump down to pick him up.

When landing fish on rock jetties and breakwaters, you need a long-handled gaff. If you are fishing alone, put the gaff within reaching distance so that you can grab it and gaff the fish. If you are with another angler, he can do the gaffing. At night, a headlight is a must in order to follow the fish near the rocks and watch where you can gaff it. Extra care must be taken when the water is rough so that you don't get too low and get washed off the jetty. All these problems and dangers offer the challenge and thrills to make surf fishing from a jetty an exciting affair.

Chapter 10

Striped Bass

The real "king of the surf" is the striped bass. The most sought and highly prized fish along the Atlantic Coast, the striper is an unpredictable, wary fish which is not too easily caught. Because it grows big enough to give the surf angler something to brag about, the man who has caught a striper of over 25 or 30 lbs. has a worthwhile trophy. Also, he can always set his sights on a bigger fish since stripers in the 60-lb. class are sometimes taken from the beaches—and they reach even a larger size. Striped bass can be caught on some kind of artificial lure, they fight hard, and they make good eating. The result is that most surf anglers would rather catch one striped bass, especially a big one, than a dozen other kinds of fish.

Unfortunately, striped bass are not too numerous compared to other surf fish. Even during the years when they are fairly plentiful they are not easy to catch. If you see a consistently successful striped bass surf angler, you can be pretty sure that the man knows his stuff and is a hard, persevering fisherman. But even the most successful surf angler soon discovers that fishing for striped bass is a "feast or famine" proposition. The surf angler will go for days without catching even a single striper, then all of a sudden things get hot and he makes a killing. Then it slows down again with perhaps two, three, or more days of slow fishing. This up-and-down cycle in surf fishing for stripers is, of course, due to weather, water, or bait conditions as discussed in Chapter 6.

Other factors also influence striped bass fishing. One example is migrations. Striped bass are found along the Atlantic Coast from Canada to Florida and, to a lesser extent, in the Gulf of Mexico. However, they are caught mostly in the surf from Maine to Delaware. In other areas they are almost strictly bay, river, and sound fish. On the West Coast in Pacific waters, surf fishing for striped bass is even more limited since they are caught mostly along a few beaches in the San Francisco area.

77

On the Atlantic Coast there are local populations of striped bass which spend the winter in rivers and bays. These fish leave these waters in the spring, show up in the surf usually around April or May, and return to the inland waters late in the fall. But another migration of striped bass also takes place from the Chesapeake Bay region, which is believed to be the main spawning area for striped bass. These fish head north in the spring and return south in the fall.

It's obvious, then, that, if the striped bass show up in large numbers in a certain area and stay there for a period of time, you will have good fishing. Just why the stripers pick a certain spot or area and stay there is not definitely known, but it's a pretty good guess that water temperatures and food have a lot to do with it. If there are plenty of crabs, worms, or baitfish in a certain area, stripers will naturally congregate there and feed as long as the food is present. If the food is scarce or the baitfish leave, the stripers probably follow them or look for other areas where food is more plentiful. Striped bass, of course, are omnivorous feeders and will eat almost any small shellfish, crustacean, or baitfish they can catch. If these foods are scarce, they won't stay long in a certain area but will move to better waters. Of course, it's true that there are always a few striped bass in almost every surf fishing spot where they are known to be caught, but these few fish rarely provide good fishing. What is needed is good-sized schools of stripers in a given area to furnish even fair fishing.

One reason for this is that even when there are plenty of striped bass along a beach and plenty of food for them, the fishing varies from day to day. Striped bass feed and gorge themselves for a day or two, then seem to fast for a few days before feeding again. If you want good fishing you must get down to the beach on the days when they are feeding actively or are on the prowl for food.

The most successful striped bass fishermen put in a lot of time fishing. They go out as often as possible, or at least every weekend, and keep in touch with the latest information on striped bass runs. Newspapers often print such news, but it is usually a day or two too late. For best results, you should get down to the beach, check for yourself, and talk with other anglers; swap information with a fishing friend; ask the local fishing tackle dealer about the latest developments on the striped bass front.

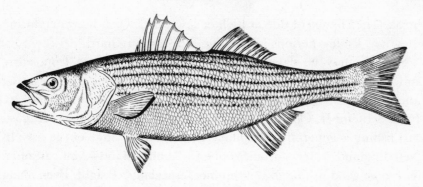

Striped Bass

When you hear about a striped bass run along a nearby beach, it pays to get there as soon as possible. Holding off for a day or two may be too late: conditions will change, the stripers will stop feeding, and you will have to wait until the next run. Timing your fishing trips is one of the real secrets of striped bass fishing success.

Even if there is a run of striped bass along a certain beach, it doesn't mean that the fish will feed all day or all night long. Stripers move in close to shore within reach of the surf angler only for short periods of time. At least, they only feed or strike for short periods while the rest of the time they are offshore in deeper water or are not actively feeding.

The most successful striper fishing specialists put in a lot of time on the beach to be there at the right time when the stripers decide to feed. Along such beaches as those found on Cape Cod, parts of Rhode Island, and Montauk Point, Long Island, you'll see anglers camped in beach buggies for a whole weekend or days at a time waiting for the best fishing periods.

The peak feeding periods of striped bass normally take place about an hour before sundown until about midnight or a bit later. Then there is usually a lull until about an hour before daybreak, when they start feeding again. Stripers will continue feeding as it gets light until two or three hours later, when the sun gets too bright and high in the sky. If the day is cloudy and the water is rough or a storm is blowing, the fishing may continue during the daytime, especially with the smaller school stripers. But if you want big stripers you will have better luck if you fish at sundown, during the night, and at daybreak. The change of tide at high or low water when it occurs during these top fishing periods is the time to fish really hard.

Stripers may be caught anytime during the season from early spring to late fall, but the best fishing usually takes place in the spring and fall runs. The top fishing months along the Atlantic Coast are June, September, October, and November. During July and August, surf fishing is generally slow along the southern range of the fish. In New England waters—from Maine to Rhode Island—you can often find some good fishing in the summer, especially at night. Even along their southern range, you can often take stripers, if you fish with such baits as seaworms, clams, shedder crabs, squid, and live eels.

When using artificial lures for striped bass, you should carry a good basic assortment to be ready for these fish. You should have metal squids of various sizes and weights, underwater and surface plugs, jigs, rigged eels, and eelskin lures. Metal squids are best when there are small baitfish around and when the water is rough. They are most effective for small stripers. Jigs are also excellent for small stripers especially around inlets or canals where the water is deep and fast. Surface plugs in the smaller sizes are used for small fish, while the larger ones are killers for big striped bass. They work best when there is some kind of large baitfish, such as mullet, menhaden, herring, whiting, or mackerel, in the surf. They are also used in such places as the Cape Cod Canal when the squid are present. Underwater plugs produce too when stripers are feeding on baitfish. If you fish mostly at night and want good-sized stripers, you can't go wrong by using rigged eels as often as possible.

Although striped bass are found in the surf along the Atlantic Coast from Maine to Delaware, certain spots produce fish more regularly than others. Included among the following are some of the top spots which produce stripers year after year.

Starting with Maine, we find that best results are obtained at Ocean Park, Old Orchard Beach, Ogunquit Beach, the entrance to York Harbor, and the mouths of such rivers as the York, Kennebec, Mousam, and Saco. Best fishing is usually from June to September.

New Hampshire has a short coastline, but some striped bass fishing can be done there. The best spots include both sides to the entrance to Hampton Harbor, Hampton River, Piscataqua River, and Seabrook Beach. Summer and fall are the best months.

Massachusetts is famous for its striper fishing. The islands of Cutty-hunk, Nantucket, and Martha's Vineyard are very good during the late spring, summer, and fall months. Cape Cod has miles of beaches and the beach buggy angler can cover most of them. Race Point and Race Point Lighthouse, Peaked Hill Bar, North Truro, Oleans, Nauset Inlet, and Monomoy Point are the more productive spots although stripers may move in anywhere along the beaches found here. The Cape Cod Canal is a great striper spot which can be fished by the surf angler. Actually there is no surf here, but the same tackle and lures are used as in surf fishing to work the strong current in the canal. The best fishing for stripers in Massachusetts is from May to October.

Rhode Island ranks first with many surf anglers as a hot spot for big stripers. The best spots are Newport, Beavertail, Narragansett, Pt. Judith, Matunuck, Charlestown Breachway, East Beach, Quon-ochontaug, Weekapaug, and Watch Hill. Block Island, which can be

The striped bass is undisputed king of the surf fish. The author holds a 24-pounder freshly caught at Montauk Point, New York.

reached by ferry from Pt. Judith, is an outstanding spot for big stripers during the summer and fall months. The best fishing in Rhode Island waters is from May to November, with September and October the two peak months.

Connecticut is better adapted for boat fishing with its many bays, inlets, and islands. Some surf fishing is done for stripers from the rocky points and beaches and mouths of rivers entering into Long Island Sound. Spring and fall months are best for shore fishing.

New York is fortunate to have Long Island with its many fine beaches and jetties. Surf anglers fish these for striped bass and the best spots include Rockaway Point and the Rockaway beaches, Silver Point Breakwater and Atlantic Beach, Long Beach, Lido Beach, Pt. Lookout, Short Beach, Jones Beach, Fire Island, Great South Beach, Westhampton Beach, Shinnecock Inlet, Hampton Beach, and Montauk Point. During the summer months most surf fishing for stripers near New York City is at night. The best months are May, June, September, and October. Montauk is tops in the fall, with October and November outstanding.

In New Jersey, starting from Sandy Hook in the north and running south to Cape May, there are miles of beaches and jetties. Parking and fishing may be restricted during the summer bathing season in many places, but there are plenty of spots to fish before and after the season and at night. The more productive ones include Sandy Hook, Seabright, Monmouth Beach, Long Branch, Elberon, Deal, Avon-by-the-Sea, Asbury Park, Shark River and Manasquan Inlets, Island Beach, Barnegat Inlet, Beach Haven, and many of the inlets and beaches from Atlantic City down to Cape May. Stripers are caught in New Jersey waters from April to November.

Most of the Delaware coastline fronts Delaware Bay, and only a short stretch of beach runs along the ocean where surf fishing is best. Here, such spots as Cape Henlopen, Rehoboth Beach, Indian River Inlet, and Bethany Beach are the best. Fishing is done from June to December.

South of Delaware only occasional stripers are taken from the surf. Most of the fishing is done for channel bass, which will be covered in the following chapter.

Chapter 11

Channel Bass

Surf anglers from Virginia south rarely catch striped bass, but they have another fish which equals the striper in size and fighting ability. This is the channel bass or red drum which is often caught along the beaches from Delaware south to Florida and in the Gulf of Mexico. At one time, big channel bass used to come up as far north as New Jersey, but now only a few stragglers are taken in the surf in northern waters.

The channel bass has many other names, such as drum, redfish, red horse, bull redfish, red bass, bar bass, and spottail. This last name is derived from the black spot at the base of the tail. Usually, there is only one spot, but some individuals may have as many as twenty-three spots on one side. The color of a channel bass is actually not red but a coppery tinge which is a dark red-brown in the larger fish and pink or pale brown in the younger specimens. They have silvery sides and white bellies.

The channel bass is not a true bass but is a member of the croaker family, which includes the drums and weakfishes. Nevertheless, it looks somewhat like a bass in general body shape. The name "channel bass" is used mostly in the north and in southern waters it is better known as the redfish.

Whatever its name, the channel bass is highly prized for its fighting ability and its large sze. Most important, it is one of the few large gamefish which can be caught frequently in the surf. The majority of the fish caught surf fishing run small, but the channel bass together with the striped bass come big and give the surf angler and his tackle a real test.

Like the striped bass, the channel bass doesn't always feed in close to shore. Sometimes he's in deeper water offshore where the surf angler can't reach him. But as a general rule, if conditions are right the channel bass will move in close to the beach within casting distance. Although they are taken when the water is rough and white, they are not a "white water" fish in the same sense as the striper. They prefer somewhat deeper holes and sloughs.

Sometimes schools of channel bass will work close to the surf and can be seen chasing baitfish on the surface or cruising or lying under the water when it is clear. However, most of the time you won't see them and must fish blind by trying the best spots. Channel bass frequent the holes and sloughs especially during the low tides. At times they will also feed on the sand bars themselves, most often at the high tides. However, they prefer the deeper holes and edges of sand bars where they cruise along in the hope of catching an unwary baitfish, crab, or other marine creatures.

Channel bass move inshore with the tide, making the incoming tide a good time to fish. During low water they seek out the holes and deep sloughs and sharply sloping beaches with deep water near shore. You may have to wade out to the sand bar and fish the outer edge during low tide. Then, as the tide comes in, you can fish the shallower spots closer to shore.

Most channel bass fishing in the surf is bottom fishing with a bait rig. The fish-finder rig is usually used with a 7/0 or 8/0 or 9/0 hook, depending on the size of the fish that are running. The hook is baited with any one of several baits, the most popular being mullet. A small whole mullet can be used or a large one can be cut into fillets or chunks. The mossbunker or menhaden is another excellent baitfish when there are not many sharks around (this bait will attract more sharks than channel bass). One of the best baits is a piece of shedder crab. They'll also take hard crabs, if you remove the top shell, and

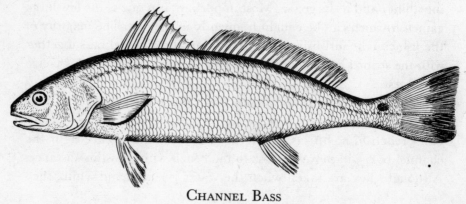

CHANNEL BASS

squid—if you can get it. Fresh squid is best but you'll also catch them on the salted variety. In fact, since most channel bass fishing is done in fairly warm climes, it's a good idea to keep the bait frozen or on ice. The next best step is to clean the bait and salt it away in a jar or other container.

I remember on one trip down to Cape Hatteras, North Carolina, when we couldn't obtain any bait for channel bass. So our native guide just took out a big jar and handed us chunks of fish that had been salted down during the previous year. I asked him what it was and he told us that the chunks were pieces of channel bass. We used them and they worked almost as well as mullet or menhaden, which are the best baits to use.

After the hook is baited, you cast out as far as you can and let it lie there a while. If no bite is felt, reel in a few feet and let it lie in the new spot for a short time. Keep repeating this until the bait is almost up on shore. If you have no bites in the same spot for a couple

William Walker (left) and G. G. Smith caught ten of these channel bass, weighing from 40 to 56 lbs., at Cape Hatteras, North Carolina—a great spot for these fish.

of hours or so, you can move up the beach and try a different area. Channel bass anglers use beach buggies and often try a few spots before they find one which produces.

When you feel a channel bass pick up the bait, you must resist the temptation to strike back. Channel bass rarely grab the bait and move off at the start. They usually fool around picking the bait up, then dropping it, picking it up, dropping it. Wait until you feel the fish take the bait before starting to move away, then set the hook firmly in the tough mouth.

Conventional tackle and the use of sinkers and baits are most practical in Atlantic waters where the channel bass run big and heavy. Heavy spinning outfits can also be used, but in many parts of Florida and in the Gulf of Mexico where channel bass run smaller and the surf is not too rough you can use lighter spin outfits and bait-casting outfits. These small channel bass also take artificial lures, such as underwater plugs, spoons, and jigs, more readily than the large channel bass in northern waters. However, there are occasions—usually when they are chasing baitfish—when the larger channel bass will also strike a metal squid, underwater plug, or large spoon.

Channel bass, especially a big one, will give you several long runs before he is licked. Let him go freely because they are a powerful fish and will break a line or even a rod if you try to check them in the beginning.

Most of the channel bass caught along their northern range will run from 15 to 30 lbs. in weight, but each year fish up to 50 and 60 lbs. or more are taken. Unless you catch a record fish it's a good idea to release the large one because channel bass in this size are coarse and make poor eating. Those under 15 lbs. are best for the table.

Channel bass may appear along any of the beaches from Delaware to the Gulf of Mexico but are most often caught in the following places. In Virginia, the beaches at Wachapreague and Chincoteague are productive spots. Paramore, Wreck, Cobb, and Smith Islands off Virginia are also good. In North Carolina, Nags Head, Oregon Inlet, Cape Hatteras, Ocracoke, Drum Inlet, and Topsail Inlet are favorite spots. In South Carolina and Georgia, most of the inlets entering into the ocean, and many of the beaches, are good places. The east coast of Northern Florida produces channel bass around the inlets and along many of the beaches. Finally, in the Gulf of Mexico chan-

The channel bass' big brother is the black drum. The young ones have stripes which make them look a little like sheepshead. These fade or disappear when the fish gets older.

nel bass are caught along the beaches, around inlets, and from the jetties.

While fishing for channel bass in the surf you'll sometimes hook and land the black drum. A close relative of the channel bass, he grows bigger, often reaching around 100 lbs. He's more sluggish and uglier, has a hump back, dirty gray-black color, and several dark stripes running down the sides from the back to the belly. The same tackle used for channel bass can be tried on the big black drum, in the surf. The smaller one can be caught with lighter spinning and bait-casting outfits. Black drum will take a hook baited with mullet, crabs, clams, and shrimp. The small black drum make fair eating, but the large ones are coarse.

The seasons vary for channel bass fishing, depending on where you are. Along the Atlantic coast the fishing starts in North Carolina sometime in April and lasts until November. The best months are April, May, October, and November. In more southerly waters, like those around Florida, the best fishing is during the fall, winter, and spring months although here they are caught all year-around in many areas.

Chapter 12

Weakfish and Bluefish

When such larger surf fish as striped bass or channel bass are scarce or refuse to bite, two other gamefish often found in the surf along the Atlantic Coast save the day on many fishing trips: the weakfish and the bluefish. Of the two, the weakfishes—both the northern and southern varieties—are usually more plentiful and easier to catch.

Let's take the northern variety of weakfish first. It is known as the common weakfish *(Cynoscion regalis)* and also as the gray weakfish, gray trout, squeteague, and salt-water trout. Found from Cape Cod to Florida, it is scarce south of the Carolinas. Arriving in northern waters during May when they appear mostly in bays and inlets, a bit later they show up along the surf and can be caught from the beaches. Some weakfish are caught all summer long from the surf, but the biggest fish are usually taken in the spring and the fall. Usually, the best fishing months are June, July, September, and October in the surf.

Since special tackle is not needed, you can use the same rod you have for surf fishing. However, the weakfish never reaches the size of the striped bass or channel bass, so a lighter tackle will provide better sport. The light and medium spinning outfits are very good to use.

During the spring run when the weakfish are feeding on baitfish, they will readily strike artificial lures. One of the best lures for them is a light, flat metal squid with a long strip of pork rind attached to the hook. A small treble hook is then slipped on the pork rind to get the fish that strike short. This metal squid is cast out and reeled very slowly with occasional speed-ups. A favorite trick with many surf anglers seeking weakfish is to cast out the metal squid and let it sink. While the lure is sinking they reel in just enough slack to keep a tight line. Often a fish will strike the metal squid as it is sinking, and a slack line will not hook them. Of course, this is a good method when fishing in deeper water.

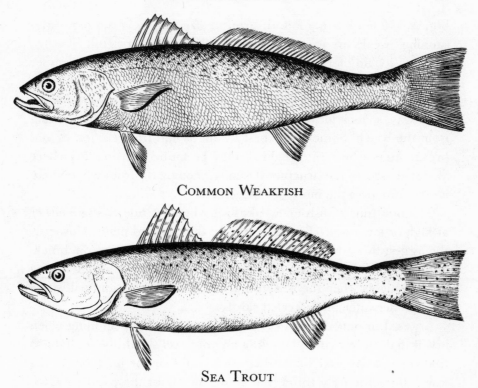

COMMON WEAKFISH

SEA TROUT

Another good lure for weakfish is a small underwater plug. I like the jointed model best since it can be reeled very slowly and you can feel it working. The plugs will take fish during the day or at night. Sometimes you will see the weakfish on the surface chasing baitfish, but most of the time you have to work your lure deep to get results.

Other lures which sometimes take weakfish include spinners, spoons, jigs, and similar artificials. However, you'll do best if you stick to light metal squids and small underwater plugs.

When the weakfish cannot be caught on artificial lures they will usually take some kind of natural bait in the surf. One of the best all-around baits for weakfish anywhere is a strip of squid. Shrimp, shedder crab, sandworms, and bloodworms will also take them. In the fall of the year, one of the best baits you can use is a strip or chunk of mullet. They'll also hit pieces of other fish, such as menhaden, mackerel, and porgies.

The same standard surf rig used for striped bass can be used for weakfish, but the hooks can be smaller if the weakfish are not too big. A 5/0 hook is a good all-around size to use. If the big "tide-running" weaks are in, you can use the larger 7/0 or 8/0 hooks.

When looking for weakfish in the surf, a good point to remember is that they like deeper and quieter water than the striped bass or channel bass. If the water is too shallow or too rough they'll usually stay away, so look for deep holes, channels, and sloughs when fishing from the beach. Some of the best fishing is had from the jetties and breakwaters where the weakfish may be found cruising anywhere along the sides of the structure. Usually, though, the front where there is a rip produces the most and biggest fish.

The best time to fish for weakfish is when the tide changes either at high or low water. They bite during the day and night. However, the largest fish are usually taken early in the morning at daybreak, in the evening, and during the night. I recall some fine fishing during moonlit nights when the weakfish are especially active and will strike small underwater plugs, reeled slowly.

A weakfish puts up a good fight especially in the beginning when it will make a few runs. The drag on your reel should be set light so that the fish can take line, otherwise you'll tear the hook out of the jaw. That's the only thing that's "weak" about them—their jaws. Always use a net or a gaff for any fish over 2 lbs.

The average weakfish will run from 1 to 5 lbs. in the surf, but the larger tide-runners will run from 6 to 8 lbs. Sometimes, larger fish in the 8- to 12-lb. class will show up although, in recent years, weakfish of all sizes have been somewhat scarce. Weakfish make fair eating, especially the smaller ones if they are prepared soon after being caught. They turn soft quickly and should be cleaned and kept on ice, or frozen.

The southern weakfish *(Cynoscion nebulosis),* also known as the sea trout, spotted weakfish, and speckled trout, is caught sometimes in the surf from Virginia south to the Gulf of Mexico. Very plentiful in Florida, it is found there in most bays, inlets, and along the beaches.

They are in southern waters most of the year but are usually caught along the surf in the Atlantic from May to December. In the Gulf of Mexico, they are also caught during the same period, in which July and August are the two good fishing months.

The southern weakfish or sea trout is often found in schools, so, if you catch one or two, the chances are excellent that more are present. They are most plentiful around inlets and on the flats and bars. Sea trout will feed on small baitfish, so shrimp and lures which imitate these are most successful. Small metal squids, spoons, jigs, and surface and underwater plugs in midget sizes work best.

When it comes to natural bait you can't beat a live shrimp for sea trout. They will also take pieces of mullet or menhaden and other fish.

The average sea trout will run from about ½ to 5 lbs. in weight in the surf. Occasionally, a larger fish will be taken, mostly around inlets, but the biggest sea trout are caught in Florida's bays and lagoons.

The bluefish is one of the gamest fish that a surf angler can catch. Of all the fish in the surf, however, the bluefish is also the most unpredictable. Certain days and seasons finds them so plentiful that anglers catch all they want of the blue choppers. Other days and seasons they are scarce. To make matters worse, bluefish are subject to cycles which result in gluts during certain years and poor fishing during others. At this time, we are in the middle of one of the gluts, and bluefish are being caught all along the Atlantic coast in great numbers. How long this will last no one really knows, but if past records are an accurate indication we can look forward to good bluefish for a dozen or more years, then about an equal period of poor fishing.

Bluefish are found in many parts of the world, and surf anglers catch them as far away as Australia. Along the Atlantic Coast they range from Nova Scotia to Brazil but are also found in the Gulf of Mexico. However, they rarely go north of Cape Cod in any numbers.

The unpredictability of bluefish discourages surf anglers from going after them deliberately unless there is a prolonged run. One day

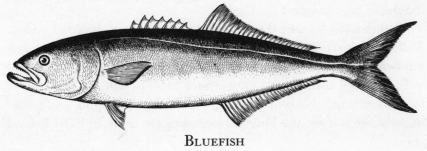

BLUEFISH

they will show up in big schools, the next day they may disappear. Along the Atlantic Coast, bluefish may show up in the surf at any time from May to November so surf anglers keep a lookout for them.

The best sign of feeding bluefish is a flock of gulls or terns diving into the water. Bluefish drive the baitfish to the surface or close to the beach, and the birds have a feast.

When there are no birds around it pays to study the water for signs of leaping baitfish or blues themselves. Bluefish, especially the smaller ones, often leap clear of the water when feeding. They are particularly active around the mouths of inlets entering the ocean, where the baitfish are swept out by the outgoing tide. Blues also like the deeper drop-offs, holes, channels, and rips—especially rips and turbulent water, where currents meet and create a choppy boil or swirling waters. However, they will also feed on sand or rock bars and other shallow spots if there are baitfish present. I've caught them on many occasions in the rough, white water stripers like. In fact, the two fish often feed together, so on one cast you may catch a bluefish and on the next a striper.

No special surf tackle is needed—use any gear you already have. For the most sport the lighter outfits, both conventional and spinning, are best.

Blues will take a wide variety of artificial lures in the surf, but the favored lure is a shiny metal squid. More have been caught on metal squids than any other single lure when surf fishing. Cast beyond or into a feeding school of blues, hold your rod tip high, and reel as fast as you can turn the reel handle.

Another fine bluefish lure is a small metal spoon heavy enough to cast with a light conventional surf rod or with a salt-water spin rod. The chrome or nickel-plated or stainless steel spoons work best and should be kept polished for blues.

Bluefish will also take the various types of jigs with bucktail, nylon, or feather skirts. They'll hit the yellow, white, and other color jigs, but here again those with chrome or nickel heads generally work best.

Plugs, both surface and underwater models, will catch plenty of bluefish at times. It's quite a thrill to use surface popping and swimming plugs and see the bluefish come up, hit them, or swirl behind them.

Other lures which often take bluefish are rigged eels and eelskin lures. However, when using a rigged eel for blues make sure it is rigged with cable wire or chain. Otherwise, a bluefish will bite through cord or line if used inside the eel. Bluefish have a habit of chopping the tail off rigged eels, so bring plenty along.

You can also catch bluefish in the surf with natural baits. They'll take pieces of menhaden, mullet, butterfish, mackerel, or small shiners and spearing or sand eels. In fact, almost any small fish can be cut and used. The regular standard surf rig is used for bluefish except that instead of using nylon for a leader you substitute wire. Bluefish will bite through nylon.

When you hook a bluefish in the surf, keep him coming at all times. If you give him any slack line he will quickly throw the hook. A favorite trick is to swim toward you at a fast speed, so you have to reel fast to avoid a slack line. Backing up the beach is considered bad form when done against any other fish, but it is often practiced when bluefishing.

After the bluefish is beached, be very careful in removing the hook. A bluefish never gives up until it dies and will continue bouncing around on shore. If he has a plug in his mouth, make sure he is firmly held or pinned down before you attempt to remove the hooks; otherwise, he may leap and drive one of the hooks into your hand. Keep your fingers out of a bluefish's mouth—their sharp teeth can give you a nasty slash.

The average-sized bluefish you catch in the surf runs from 2 to 6 lbs., but sometimes large fish in the 6- to 12-lb. class are taken. Whatever the size, they all fight hard and there's no fish in the sea that will give you the satisfying scrap that a bluefish will. For its size it has the most power, strength, and endurance, and only a jack crevalle of the same size will give you a longer fight. But then, the jack crevalle won't leap out of the water like a blue—and he doesn't taste as good.

Chapter 13

Other Surf Fishes

One fascinating thing about surf fishing is that when you cast a lure or bait out into the water, you never can be sure what you'll catch. Of course, most of the time you will be going after a certain species of fish, but you never know when a different kind will suddenly appear in the surf. The experienced surf angler is familiar with most of the fish which can be caught in his area, and he learns which lures, baits, and rigs to use for them. In this section we will discuss many of these other fish.

KINGFISH

The proper name for this fish is northern whiting *(Menticirrhus saxatilis)*, but most surf anglers in New York and New Jersey waters call it the kingfish. Found from Cape Ann to Florida, it is most numerous from New York to Virginia.

The kingfish first appears in great numbers in the surf during May and remains until September or October. The best fishing months are usually June, July, and September.

In the surf, it often comes in close to the beach in search of small worms, snails, shrimp, sand bugs, and other shellfish. It frequents the deeper holes, edges of sand bars, and channels. Some of the best fish-

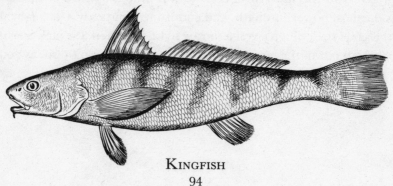

KINGFISH
94

ing can be had from jetties and breakwaters in deeper water near the end. Because they bite all day or night and during most tides, it is a common sight to see surf anglers fishing for kings at all hours during the summer months.

Although they are often caught on heavy surf tackle, the lightest rods should be used since they rarely reach more than 2 or 3 lbs. in weight. A long, limber spinning rod is ideal.

Kingfish have a small mouth and No. 1/0 O'Shaughnessy or Eagle Claw hooks, baited with bloodworms, sandworms, or bits of shrimp— the top baits—should be used. Shedder crabs and clams, sometimes strips of squid, and also sand bugs will take them.

The kingfish gives a very rapid, sharp bite—a sort of series of sharp tugs. The angler should strike back immediately to set the hook and simultaneously be prepared for the small kingfish to put up a surprising fight. After he has a good mess of fish, he can look forward to some good eating because their flesh is firm and delicious.

The southern kingfish or southern whiting *(Menticirrhus americanus)* resembles the northern kingfish a lot. Found from New Jersey to Texas but most common from Virginia to Florida, they are also caught along the beaches on many of the baits used for the northern kingfish.

Along the Pacific Coast, the California corbina *(Menticirrhus undulatus)* is a close relative of the Atlantic kingfish or whiting. It reaches a slightly larger size, however, with specimens up to 4 lbs. and even larger.

The California corbina is found along the beaches from Pt. Conception south into the Gulf of California. They are caught throughout the year in many areas, but in California the best fishing usually takes place during the summer months. They are caught on surf fishing tackle with rigs using 4-ft. nylon leaders and No. 1 or 2 hooks. The best baits are pile worms, rock worms, sand crabs, mussels, clams, and shrimp.

CROAKERS

The croaker family is a large one and includes the weakfishes, channel bass, drums, and many other fishes. Along the Pacific Coast

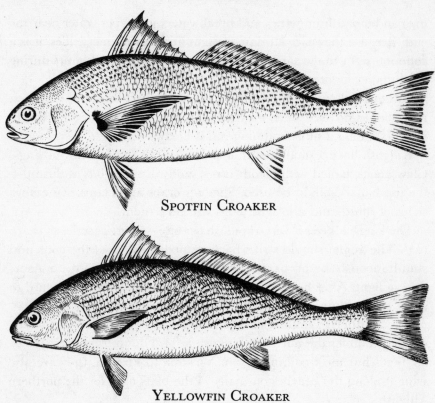

SPOTFIN CROAKER

YELLOWFIN CROAKER

the most popular croaker caught in the surf is the spotfin croaker *(Roncador stearnsi),* which is found from Point Conception to Baja, California. It is caught throughout the year but is most plentiful during the late summer and fall months.

Although the spotfin croaker averages from 1 to 3 lbs., fish up to 5 or 6 lbs. are often taken. Its topmost weight is 9¼ lbs. Most of the surf fishing is done in so-called "croaker holes" deep spots and channels near shore.

Small No. 1 or 1/0 hooks are used, which are baited with either pile worms, sand worms, soft-shell sand crabs, mussels, pieces of clam, or shrimp. The spotfin croaker hits the bait hard and when hooked puts up a good fight for its size. Care should be taken to play the fish carefully, since its mouth is easily torn and any slack line will cause the hook to fall out.

The other croaker which is found in the same area as the spotfin is the yellowfin croaker *(Umbrina roncador).* It is much smaller, however, rarely attaining more than 3 lbs. in weight. Hooks in sizes No. 1 or 2 may be used, but many of the same baits used for the spotfin croaker will work. In addition, small anchovies and pieces of other fishes are recommended.

Along the Atlantic Coast the common croaker *(Micropogon undulatus)* is sometimes taken in the surf, although fishing is better for them from piers or boats. They rarely reach more than 4 or 5 lbs. in weight so No. 1 or 1/0 hooks are used. The best baits for them are seaworms, clams, shrimp, squid, and bits of shedder crab.

There is fishing for croakers along the Atlantic Coast from Delaware to the Gulf of Mexico. A few croakers are found farther north, but the best fishing is from Virginia south. Croakers bite during the day and night, with the early morning, evening, and night hours being very productive.

BLACKFISH

The blackfish or tautog is not a true surf fish, but it has saved many a day for surf anglers fishing in New England, New York, and New Jersey. They come close to shore along rocky areas and feed near jetties and breakwaters, so they are within reach of the surf angler.

Blackfish are found from Canada to South Carolina but are most common from Cape Cod to New Jersey. They come close to shore in the spring in late April or early May and bring about good fishing during May and June. In the summer, the smaller blackfish are caught

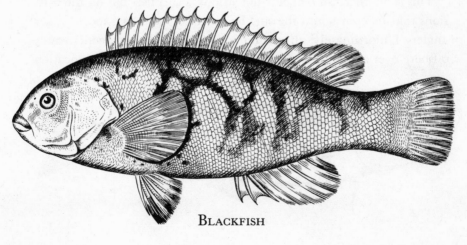

BLACKFISH

near the shore but the larger ones leave for deeper water. Then in the fall, starting in September and up until November, the big ones come back close to shore and the best fishing takes place during these months.

You can use your regular conventional surf rod for blackfish. Spinning rods are not too good unless you use very strong lines. However, they can be used on mussel beds or oyster beds where there are no rocks. Nevertheless, the best blackfishing takes place around rocks and here you need a stiff rod and strong line. The best hook to use is a Virginia in No. 6 for average-sized fish and No. 4 for larger fish.

The rocky shores of Massachusetts, Rhode Island, Connecticut, and the jetties of Long Island and New Jersey offer good fishing. Blackfish feed in compact schools and a large number will gather in a good spot. The angler who locates one of these spots has the advantage. He may take several blackfish while other anglers a few feet away may have little or no luck, so it pays to try several holes until one which produces is found.

The best baits for blackfish are fiddler crabs, green crabs, hermit crabs, sand bugs, sandworms, and clams. Blackfish are very clever at stealing the bait so bring along plenty of bait and rigs. You'll lose a lot of sinkers and hooks when fishing for them, but it's a price you must pay if you want to catch blackfish.

POLLOCK

This is another fish which is not strictly a surf fish, but on the occasions that he comes into the surf he furnishes some fast sport for surf anglers. Unfortunately, although the pollock is found in deeper waters offshore over a wide area, he is caught only in a few favored locations

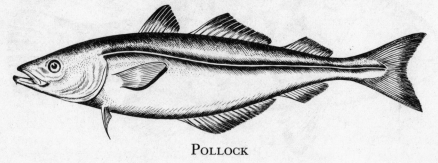

POLLOCK

Courtesy The Salt Water Sportsman

Pollock similar to this one are often landed at Race Point, Provincetown, Massachusetts, in May. The rig is a wood splasher with bucktail jig.

by surf anglers. Three spots that often produce pollock fishing in the surf consistently are Race Point on Cape Cod, Massachusetts; Pt. Judith in Rhode Island; and Montauk Point on Long Island. Even at these spots the best fishing is usually for short periods in the spring, around May, and again in the late fall in October and November.

Pollock are active, streamlined members of the codfish family that feed often on smaller baitfish. They chase the baitfish to the surface early in the morning at daybreak and at dusk. This is the time surf anglers take them by casting small metal squids, spoons, jigs, and plugs. One of the best lures is the splasher wood block with a tiny spoon or jig behind it.

Although pollock don't fight as long or as hard as striped bass or channel bass, they are easier to catch in large quantities and also run to a good size. In Massachusetts waters, a 20- or 30-lb. pollock is an average fish during the spring runs which take place there.

Pollock make fair eating and are somewhat similar to cod or had-
dock in taste and texture. If there is a good run of these fish you can
easily catch enough to freeze for months to come.

FLUKE AND FLOUNDERS

These members of the flatfish family are sometimes taken in the
surf. The flounder most often caught by surf anglers along the Atlantic
Coast is the fluke or summer flounder *(Paralichthys dentatus)*. The
fluke is a large, active flounder found from Cape Cod to the Carolinas—mostly in bays, inlets, and deeper waters a short distance from
shore in the ocean. However, it sometimes comes into the surf, especially during the summer months and early fall when it is caught
from the beaches.

Fluke strike on a wide variety of baits, such as seaworms, squid,
clams, and smaller fishes. The most extensively used bait is a live kil-
liefish used in combination with a strip of squid. After you catch your
first fluke, you can cut a strip from its belly and use that.

When fishing for fluke, you generally use about a 5/0 long shank
hook on a 3-ft. leader tied just above the sinker. The hook is baited,
cast out as far as possible, and reeled in slowly to give the bait some
movement. Because fluke will hit a moving bait more readily than a
stationary one, they are sometimes taken on artificial lures in the
surf. The best lures are light metal squids, jigs, and underwater plugs,
but fluke will also hit spoons, which can be used with spin outfits.
The thing to remember when using such artificials is that fluke will
strike a slow-moving lure more often than a fast-moving one.

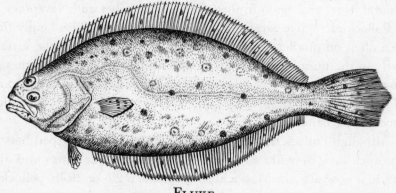

FLUKE

The average fluke caught will run from 1 to 3 lbs., but the bigger "doormats" often run up to 12, 14, or more pounds. The world's rod and reel record is a 20-lb. fish.

The winter flounder *(Pseudopleuronectes americanus)* is smaller than the fluke in size and less active. It is occasionally caught by surf anglers in the spring and fall, usually around inlets. The best bait to use is a piece of sandworm or bloodworm, clam, or mussel.

Along the Pacific Coast another member of the flounder family— the California halibut—sometimes ventures close to shore and can be taken by surf or shore anglers. However, fishing is better for them in deeper water reached from piers and boats.

POMPANO

In southern waters the most highly prized fish caught in the surf is the pompano. In fact, there are many so-called "pompano men" who specialize in this fishing and neglect all the other species. When there is a run of pompano along the beaches, you will find these men joined by other surf anglers competing for this popular fish.

The pompano is found along the Atlantic Coast from the Carolinas to the Gulf of Mexico, as well as along the coasts of Brazil and in parts of the Carribean. However, the best fishing in United States waters is found in Florida where they usually start running along the east coast of Florida, around February, and continue to be fairly plentiful until the summer months.

In the surf, pompano are found close to the beach when there is

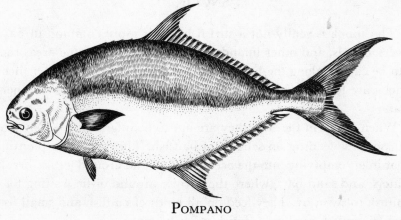

POMPANO

some rough water to activate the surf and wash out the small crabs and crustaceans the fish feed on. When there are many sand bars and shallow spots, the high tides are usually best. In deeper waters they can be caught at the low tides, but the incoming tide is generally preferred.

Although many anglers use regular surf rods for this fishing, a lighter rod and line is more suitable. Pompano fight hard for their size, but the average fish caught will run from 1 to 3 lbs. so light tackle provides more fun. A salt-water spinning outfit using a 12- or 15-lb. test line and some light sinkers is ideal, but a pyramid or round sinker can be used. Small No. 1 or 2 hooks are rigged above the sinker.

The top bait for pompano is a sand bug (these are described in the chapter on natural baits). The pompano hits the bait, mouths it, and takes off in a hurry, so that there's no mistaking a strike from a pompano. Then, when they are hooked, they use their broad sides effectively in putting up a good scrap.

Pompano can also be caught on small artificial lures, such as tiny plugs, spoons, and spinners, but the most effective artificial lure is a small jig with yellow or white bucktail or feathers. These lures are worked slowly and erratically close to the bottom.

After you catch some pompano you have one of the finest eating fish in the sea. They bring a fancy price in the market or restaurant so don't give them away. Broil or bake them and then you'll know why surf anglers would rather catch pompano than any other fish.

SNOOK

The snook is really not a surf fish but is more common in bays, rivers, canals, and other inland waters. However, in some areas they can be caught along the beaches, and then surf anglers go after them. Snook are found in Florida, the Gulf of Mexico, and other southern waters.

When found in the surf, they are apt to be migrating for spawning purposes or feeding on schools of baitfish. They are most plentiful near inlets emptying into the ocean or Gulf and around jetties, breakwaters, and sand bars, where they cruise around or lie waiting for a baitfish to swim by. They feed on all kinds of baitfish and small fish, such as mullet, sardines, pinfish, and shrimp.

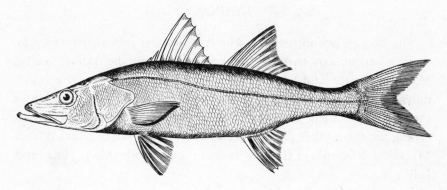

SNOOK

Although the snook is not a true surf fish like the striped bass, he has many similarities to this fish. The snook, like the striper, is often found around such obstructions as bridge and pier piles, in fast currents, and rips around sand bars. He does a lot of feeding at dawn, dusk, and during the night.

The smaller snook or average-sized fish runs from about 2 to 5 lbs. The larger ones run anywhere from 8 to 10 lbs. up to 30 and can grow to more than 50 lbs. When the smaller fish are around, a light conventional or medium spin rod is best. If big snook are present, especially in areas with obstructions around, a heavy spin rod or conventional rod is more practical.

Snook will take a wide variety of artificial lures. The most productive type of plug is a surface model which can be jerked to simulate a wounded mullet or other baitfish. They'll also take underwater plugs, metal squids, spoons, jigs, and eelskin lures. When artificial lures fail to produce, you can try such natural baits as live baitfish or shrimp. A hooked snook puts up a wild and determined battle, and even the smaller ones will leap and thrash around on top of the water. The favorite trick of the bigger ones, which give long runs, is to try to foul or cut the line on a bridge or pier pile, in mangrove roots, or other obstruction.

Snook make good eating. The smaller ones should be filleted, whereas the larger ones can be cut into steaks. They have a white, firm meat with a fine flavor.

Snook have been made a gamefish in Florida waters so check the size limit and bag limit before you fish for them.

TARPON

The tarpon is another fish which is not a true surf fish since he doesn't particularly care for breakers but prefers the quieter waters of rivers, canals, and bays. However, in some areas they are sometimes found in the surf along the beaches, especially where rivers enter the ocean and along many beaches in the Gulf of Mexico. The best fishing for them takes place in Florida and the Gulf of Mexico from March to November; the best months are usually May, June, and July.

Tarpon are often found in large schools and can be seen rolling on the surface. The surf angler will find his best fishing from shore at river mouths and also from jetties and breakwaters. For real sport, surf anglers use spinning outfits, but if the fish are big they lose many. A conventional surf rod will hold and land more of the larger fish, especially if natural baits are used. These are swallowed and the tarpon is hooked more securely. With artificial lures many fish fail to get hooked or are hooked lightly and get rid of the lure on the first jump.

Tarpon are, of course, noted for their high leaps into the air. They shake their heads, land with a loud splash, and fight hard right up until the end. The fact that the average fish will run from 20 to 80 lbs. makes the tarpon a prized trophy. Fish over 100 lbs. are often caught because they grow to 300 lbs.

Tarpon will strike such artificial lures as surface plugs, underwater plugs, spoons, and jigs. They'll take natural baits, such as live and dead mullet, pinfish, and catfish, as well as shrimp and crabs.

The trick is to make a tarpon strike the artificial or take the natural bait. Although they are often seen swimming or rolling on the surface,

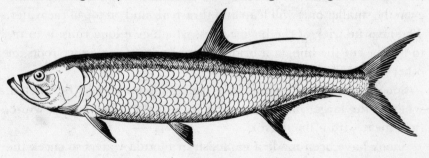

TARPON

they are not always in a feeding mood. You need persistence here and must keep on casting lures and changing lures until the fish decide to cooperate. Usually, the best fishing takes place early in the morning, at dusk, and during the night.

SHARKS AND RAYS

Not too many surf anglers deliberately fish in the surf for sharks or rays, which are usually regarded as pests. Surf anglers using light or medium surf rods or spin rods have a poor chance of landing these fish, so when they appear many anglers either quit fishing or continue to lose rigs and line to these heavy, powerful brutes.

If you want some fun and a good workout, though, try catching these fish, especially the sharks, from the beach. The heavy conventional surf rod and a big reel holding 300 or 400 yds. of line is best. A line testing 45 or 60 lbs. will give you a better chance of landing a big shark. An important item in shark fishing is the wire leader, which should be at least 6 ft. long and made of cable or stainless steel wire. To the end of this leader a strong 9/0 or 10/0 hook is fastened.

Since it is difficult to cast such a leader any distance, some surf anglers lay out the long leader on the beach and heave it out a good length. Other anglers coil the wire leader and tie it with a weak cord. When a shark strikes, the cord breaks and the leader straightens out.

The best shark fishing in the surf takes place around inlets and river mouths and along the sharply sloping beaches with deep water near shore. In northern Atlantic waters, shark fishing is best during the summer months; in southern waters, they are often taken the year round.

One of the best shark baits is a big chunk, or a whole, menhaden because the oily flesh attracts the sharks. Almost any other fish can also be cut up and used for bait. A shark doesn't fool around too long with a bait—he quickly gulps it and takes off on a steady run. The angler sets the hook and the fight is on.

Depending on the size of the fish, the battle may last from half an hour to two hours or more. Sharks and rays are not spectacular fighters unless you happen to hook a mako or a spinner shark, which are rarely taken inshore anyway. Most of the sharks caught along the Atlantic Coast will be the brown, hammerhead, and nurse sharks.

Although not spectacular or fast, sharks do have plenty of power and endurance. The secret in battling them lies in not allowing them any rest. As soon as the run ends and the fish tries to sulk on the bottom, start working to keep him moving. Bring your rod tip back sharply several times in succession. Sometimes if you tighten your line and pluck it with your fingers, you may start the fish moving again. If the shark is small or medium-sized you can often pump him in slowly. Big sting rays will give you a lot of trouble in this respect because their broad, flat surfaces enable them to hug the sand bottom and create a powerful suction.

The most crucial part of the fight is beaching a big shark or ray. Then the weight of the fish comes into play, and if the surf is rough you will have your hands full. A long-handled gaff is an aid if you are fishing with another angler. Then he can wade out and gaff the fish and both anglers can drag him out on the beach. Care should always be taken when fishing for sharks—their sharp teeth can produce a nasty wound. The same is true of a sting ray's tail with its barb so keep away from these weapons.

There are many other fishes which are occasionally caught in the surf. Several members of the mackerel family sometimes come close to shore and are taken from high rocks, jetties, and breakwaters. In Florida and other warm waters, the jack crevalle is often caught off the beaches and from jetties. In California waters, such fish as the yellowtail, the various rockfishes, and surf perches are taken from the surf or rocky shores. Farther north in Oregon and Washington, anglers fishing in the surf at river mouths catch salmon and steelhead.

The angler will find that methods and techniques used in surf fishing are pretty much the same all over the country. If a man is a good surf angler in his own area, he can be pretty certain of catching fish in other sections of the country. Naturally, he may have to watch and study the natives to find the proper bait or lure which the fish are taking and the best time to use it. The natives also have the advantage in that they know the best spots through years of fishing, but the visiting angler can locate them if he uses his knowledge of surf conditions and applies it to the new territory.

Chapter 14

Angler's Workshop

Surf fishing is hard on tackle because salt water corrodes or rusts metal on reels and sand, rocks, and barnacles wear lines. The constant casting with artificial lures also wears reels and guides on rods. The glass rods used today require less maintenance than the old bamboo rods of the past, but, in order to get the maximum use from your tackle, proper care is necessary. This requires little time, and the angler should get into the habit of working on his tackle at the end of each fishing trip.

Your fishing rod should be examined before the start of the fishing season. The heat and dryness of steam-heated apartments and rooms often loosens the ferrules or the reel seat, which can usually be made tight again by merely reheating the metal over a gas stove or an alcohol lamp. First you remove the ferrule or reel seat from the rod and heat the ferrule over a flame until it is very hot. Take a stick of ferrule cement and heat it over the flame, too. Now spread the cement over the spot where the ferrule or reel seat originally was. Do this while holding the rod high over the flame so that the cement remains in a liquid state. Then force the ferrule back into place. If it doesn't go on easily, hold it over the flame and then try it. The same thing can be done with a top guide. If there is a lot of play between the ferrule or reel seat and the wood part it fits over, you may have to lay a few strands of cord over the wood to insure a tight fit.

If any of the guides are loose on your rod or if your rod requires a complete overhaul, you can strip the guides off and rewind the rod. (Of course, if you haven't got the time or the inclination, you can have any tackle store do it for you. But it isn't difficult and many surf anglers do their own rod winding.) The first step is to remove the old silk or nylon wrappings and varnish. Cut the windings with a razor blade or sharp knife and peel them off. The old varnish can be removed with fine steel wool, but, previous to this, the old guides should be marked with crayon or pencil for locating later.

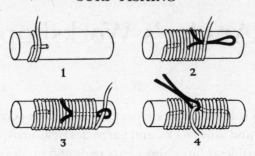

STEPS IN ROD-WINDING

The rod is now ready for winding. A straight winding is very simple and offers little difficulty. The silk or nylon rod winding thread comes in different sizes and colors. Number A is often used but is rather fine and is best for the lighter rods. Number D is thicker in diameter and is easier and quicker to wind.

The only trick to rod winding is the beginning and the ending of the wrapping. To begin the winding, tuck the end of the thread under the first few turns and continue the wrapping until the end of the thread is buried. To finish off a winding, take a short separate piece of thread, make a loop, and then, when you have a few more turns to complete the winding, place this separate piece of thread over the end of the winding with the loop facing out and past the last turn. Now wind several more turns over the loop and thread the end through the eye of the loop. Take the two protruding ends of the buried loop and pull the end of the wrapping under the last turn, which leaves the end buried under the winding. (See also the illustrations in this chapter.)

Next take a comb or a round piece of plastic or celluloid and rub the round side over the wrapping to flatten the thread and close up any spaces between the strands. Now get some color preservative and apply it over the silk or nylon thread. Two or three coats should be given, allowing each to dry first. This is done to preserve the natural colors of the winding when the rod is varnished.

After the preservative is dry, the rod is ready for its first coat of varnish. Use a flat soft brush and apply a light coat, preferably in a warm room free from dust. After the first coat is dry, the rod should be rubbed down with fine steel wool. (This is done after each coat— it may take five or more coats of varnish to complete the job.)

Many surf anglers also make their own rods. Actually, all they do is assemble the rods from parts which can be bought in many fishing tackle stores or order the rod parts by mail from companies making glass rod blanks. Many of these companies put out complete kits containing all the parts necessary to assemble a conventional or spinning surf rod. They supply the instructions, too, and almost anyone can make up such a rod to save a few dollars.

The angler who is handy with tools can also make his own lures, such as metal squids, jigs, and plugs. Most surf anglers who do this copy existing models of lures and modify them in size and color to suit individual needs and preferences. To make an original metal squid, first carve it from some soft wood or mold it from clay. Then a plaster cast is made from this pattern, and the cast is sent to a foundry where a bronze mold can be poured.

If you'd like to copy a metal squid you already have, first start by cutting off the hook with a hacksaw or file. Then file off the rough edges and polish the squid with fine steel wool. Give the squid a light coat of vaseline so that the plaster will not adhere to it. Now you construct a small wooden frame out of thin wood, although you can also use a small cardboard box such as wooden plugs are sold in. This frame or box should be wide enough and long enough to clear the squid by at least ½ in. all around when it is placed inside. If you are using a wood frame box you don't need a bottom. Instead, get a flat piece of glass or metal and lay it flat on a table then anchor the wooden frame box on to the glass or metal with clay or putty on the outside. Place the metal squid in the center of the frame with the flat side facing down and the keel up. Make sure the tail-end of the squid

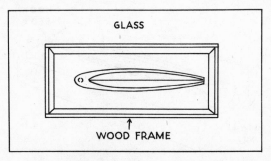

METAL SQUID READY TO BE CAST

(where the hook was) is only about ¼ in. away from the frame. Mix some plaster of Paris in a small pot or can. When you mix the plaster break up all the lumps by feeling around with your fingers. This is important, for otherwise the cast will be imperfect. Now pour the plaster into the frame until the squid is buried by at least ½ in. Then wait for the plaster to harden.

After about 15 or 20 minutes break open the frame or box and turn over the cast. With the point of a knife loosen the squid from the cast and take it out carefully in order not to damage the plaster. It will take several days for the cast to dry, unless you speed it up by baking it in an oven.

As soon as it is dry, carve a pouring hole in the head end of the cast—the front where the eye will go. Then you cut out a small slot for the hook on the other end. The plaster cast can be used as a temporary mold with a flat section of metal or plaster placed against it. You can use block tin melted in a ladle with some lead added to it but make sure the plaster cast is thoroughly dry before pouring, or else the molten metal will splatter in all directions. You can pour anywhere from 6 to 12 metal squids with such a plaster cast before it starts breaking up.

To make a permanent mold, do not use the plaster cast but send it to a foundry and have a bronze copy made. When this mold comes back it is rough and requires some finishing, which can be done with a flat file on the outside surfaces and with small three-cornered and pointed files on the inside of the mold. If you have one of those small hand-grinding tools, you can use that to take off the rough surfaces. Finish the job with emery cloth and then polish with crocus cloth.

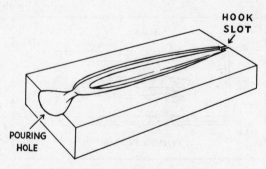

FINISHED PLASTER CAST

Next, cut a slot in the tail-end of the mold for the hook or eye, depending on whether you want a stationary or swinging hook. This holds the hook in place when pouring and should be a tight fit. Finally, get a flat metal plate the same size as the mold to use as a cover. If you have the necessary tools, you can fasten hinges to the cover and mold and add two handles. In the meantime, you can use the mold if you get a small clamp to keep the cover in place while pouring.

You can also make plaster or bronze molds to cast jigs, except that you must cast two parts to make the mold. First, you make a small wooden frame or get a small cardboard box, fill this half full with plaster of Paris, and take the jig pattern you are copying and sink it halfway in the wet plaster. Next, insert two nails with flat heads into the plaster in opposite corners. They will act as locating pins when putting the two halves of the cast together.

After the first pouring of the plaster sets, coat the exposed parts with heavy oil and pour the other half of the cast into the cardboard box. After this plaster sets, break apart the box, remove the cast, and, to separate the two halves, pry with a knife at the line where the two casts meet. Now put the two plaster casts aside to dry for a week or more.

When the plaster casts are dry, carve a pouring hole at the head of the jig, a groove to take the wire eyelet on top, and a slot to take the hook at the tail end. This must be done in both plaster casts. To pour, you place the hook in the slot and fashion an eyelet from heavy brass or copper wire and put it into the slot, so that the two ends stick into the mold.

You can use block tin or lead to pour the jig. Block tin makes a lighter, shiny jig, but lead makes a heavier jig which must be painted. When pouring, hold the two plaster halves with a glove. The pouring hole will be on top, of course, and the hook on the bottom.

After the jigs or metal squids are cast, you can tie bucktail, feathers, or nylon around the hook. Yellow, white, red, and orange feathers or bucktail are usually used—wrapped around the hook with heavy thread which is then coated with quick drying cement. The jig heads can be painted to match the colors of the feathers or bucktail.

Many surf anglers also make their own wooden plugs. If you have a lathe you can easily turn down all the plugs you need. The best wood for plugs is cedar because it is easy to work, resists moisture, and floats with added weight of hooks and metal parts. However, you can also use other woods, such as ash, cypress, or birch.

The quick way to fasten hooks to a plug is by means of screw eyes, but they should have a long thread and be thick and strong enough to hold a big fish. For salt-water use, bass screw eyes are best since they do not rust.

A more secure method of fastening is to use a brass saddle or hook hanger which has two eyes, one on each end to take two small screws. Such saddles can easily be made from a strip of brass about ¼ in. wide and about ¹⁄₃₂ in. thick. You can use pliers to bend a half-circle that will take the hook and to drill two holes for the screw eyes.

If you have a spray gun you can use that to paint the plug, which is done best with lacquers before assembling the hooks and other parts. However, you can assemble the plug and enamel it with a brush. First, coat the plug with a basic coat of white enamel or lacquer then add the other colors.

One important consideration when making any lures is to buy the strongest and best hooks possible. Get cadmium-plated or tinned hooks whenever possible because hooks with these two finishes last longer than others before rusting. Make sure they are of extra heavy wire—surf fish often run big and will straighten out a weak, thin wire hook.

After each fishing trip, your tackle requires some care to keep it in good shape. The rod should be removed from the bag or container and can be washed with a damp rag, then wiped with a dry one. The guides, especially, should be washed with fresh water to prevent corrosion.

Reels, both conventional and spinning types, should either be washed in lukewarm fresh water or wiped with a damp rag, then worked over with an oil-soaked rag. For a thorough cleaning, you can wash the reel in kerosene, using a stiff brush to get into the corners and tight spots. All the moving parts and bearings which require oil or grease should be attended to. Special notice should be given to the bearings in which the spool revolves in conventional reels: these require oil before and during each fishing trip. In spinning reels, the line roller and the handle knob require oil often.

At the end of each fishing season, it's a good idea to send your reel to the factory for a complete checkup and overhaul if necessary. As a result, you are set for the coming fishing season and assured of a good working reel which won't let you down when you need it most.

Fishing lines today require less care than the older linen lines of the past. They don't have to be dried after each fishing trip, but they should be examined carefully before using to see if they have been cut, frayed, or weakened in any way.

Always examine the hooks and fastenings on your lures to see that they are not badly rusted or weak. Badly rusted hooks, as well as leaders and snaps, can often be changed on many plugs. If they are old and kinked or badly corroded, change them before you go fishing.

All this tackle care will pay off in the long run. When hooking a big fish in the surf, it's comforting to know that your fishing tackle is in good condition. The careless or lazy angler who neglects his fishing tackle often ends up losing a big fish—one that he may have spent years searching for—so give your surf fishing tackle the good care it should be given.

Chapter 15

Sportsmanship and Conservation

Surf anglers these days are confronted by many problems: growing population, expanding cities and suburbs, network of highways, and similar developments have created many. The number of surf anglers, for example, has increased tremendously in recent years. It wasn't too long ago that a surf angler could go down to the beach, even on a weekend, and find plenty of fishing room, but today he runs into many other surf anglers looking for a spot to fish. On weekends and holidays, most of our popular surf fishing spots are crowded—so crowded, in fact, that it takes much of the enjoyment out of surf fishing.

What makes the problem even worse is that, although the number of surf anglers increases, the beach area where surf fishing can be done decreases. Now, you run into many beaches which are fenced off and surrounded by such signs as "No Trespassing," "Private Property," "Keep Off," and "No Fishing." The developments by cities, towns, and private individuals are slowly taking over our wilder beaches. Today, instead of finding sand dunes and miles of uninhabited beaches, the surf angler is more apt to be fishing with boardwalks, hotels or apartments, homes, highways, and other signs of civilization in the background. Only a few beaches are still wild, and these are threatened by future developments.

During the summer months the surf angler is also constantly harassed by bathers, lifeguards, and police when he tries to fish during the daytime. The result is that he is forced to fish late at night or very early in the morning. Even along the beaches where he can fish unmolested, he often finds parking is a big problem. If he tries to find a spot near the fishing area, he often runs into restricted zones and "No Parking" signs.

Not only are the beaches shrinking, but also the spread of cities and towns has resulted in the filling in and draining of marshes and bays. Such waters provide a sanctuary for the young gamefish and baitfish. As more and more such inland waters are filled in or drained, the result will be fewer and fewer fish.

Pollution has also taken its toll of gamefish and reduced the total fishing area. Many beaches near our largest cities and towns are so badly polluted that fish avoid them. Such fish as striped bass also enter rivers in search of brackish and fresh water for spawning purposes. If the mouths of these rivers are badly contaminated, they act as barriers to the fish. Dams, too, prevent fish from going up rivers to their spawning grounds.

Commercial fishing continues to deplete the number of surf fish in many areas. In recent years, more and more Atlantic states have passed laws protecting the striped bass against netting. The snook has also been made a gamefish in Florida, but, as both the sports and commercial fishermen continue to catch certain species, the supply is sure to diminish and result in poor fishing.

There are no easy solutions to these problems. Many coastal states have started research projects in an effort to find the answers. When they do get them and offer programs or suggest steps to be taken in correcting the situations above, they should get the full support of all surf anglers. Such action can be effected through the many surf fishing clubs and other sportsmen's organizations.

There's no doubt that the increase in surf anglers and the decrease in fishing area have resulted in crowded conditions along many of our beaches. This calls for more sportsmanship among our surf anglers. Unfortunately, the misconduct of many newcomers to the sport has often spoiled the fishing for other anglers. Friction, arguments, and even fights have sometimes arisen.

Every surf angler should try to live up to the unwritten laws of the sport. One of these is that the man who arrives first on the scene is entitled to his spot. Many surf anglers, especially beginners, have no idea how much space is required for safe and comfortable surf fishing. Along an open beach, he should stand at least 50 ft. away from the nearest surf angler. Those who have done a lot of pier fishing or boat fishing, especially party boat fishing, wonder why so much room is needed in surf fishing. Well, when casting lures or bait, a surf angler doesn't always want to cast directly in front of him. Every once in a while he likes to make a cast at an angle to the left or right. Also, if a strong wind is blowing, his cast or his neighbor's cast may land far to the left or right, perhaps causing tangled lines with another angler close by. If a big fish is hooked, he may start running sharply to the left or right, run into the line of a nearby angler, and escape.

Therefore, another rule in surf fishing is that if the angler next to you hooks a fish, you should reel in your line to allow him to play the fish. If you are fishing some distance from the angler who has the fish on, you can usually reel in your line in time. But if you are close to the other angler, the fish may run into your line before you get a chance to reel in. Give the other fellow as much room as you can along an open beach, because, with miles of beach, there's no reason to crowd a surf angler.

When it comes to fishing from jetties and breakwaters some crowding is often unavoidable, especially if there are only one or two jetties in the vicinity. Even along beaches where there are dozens of jetties, some thoughtless surf anglers insist on crowding other anglers. Here the rule is that if there are one or two anglers on the end of a jetty, you should not try to fish there also. Most jetties and breakwaters are narrow, and there is room only for one or two men up front to cast. The best policy is to stay off that jetty and go to the next one. If there are no other jetties around and if you must fish from that jetty, you should stand about 30 or more feet from the end of the structure in back of the angler or anglers in front. Other anglers arriving should fall a similar distance behind those already up front. If you insist on going up to the front and standing only a few feet away from the other angler you're asking for trouble—casting is difficult in such close quarters and you may get a hook from a squid or a plug in some part of your body.

Some surf anglers will say, "But the other angler or anglers have the best spot—they are catching all the fish and we aren't getting anything. I have a right to fish there as much as anyone else." That is no excuse for bad manners or poor sportsmanship. When the fish are running, they usually spread out along the beach and the chances are just as good, if not better, farther down the line. Besides, in certain spots there is just enough room for one or two anglers. If it isn't crowded they'll do all right, but if more anglers try to crowd into that spot they may ruin the fishing for everybody.

Many anglers who haven't done much surf fishing fail to appreciate the benefits and appeal of the sport. One of the basic appeals in surf fishing is that you have plenty of elbow room, water to fish, and solitude. You get a chance to relax—to feel the wind blowing in your face and to watch and hear the booming surf. The reason many surf anglers come down to the beach is to get away from highway traffic, crowded subways and trains, and people. There are times when a man wants to be alone to meditate, relax, and forget about business, job, or personal worries. Surf fishing can offer all of these, but not when other anglers insist on crowding those already there. Then you can't call it surf fishing any more; in fact, you might as well be on a crowded party boat, bridge, or pier—pushing, shouting, tangling lines, and having a hectic time. If you like such fishing and crowds, then stick to party-boat fishing or pier fishing. Should you want the restful solitude of surf fishing, learn to respect the fishing rights of others.

Because of this overcrowding and the uncertain success of surf fishing, many veteran surf anglers tend to be reticent and seem to be unsocial. If they have caught some fish in a certain spot, they keep it a secret. They know that once the word is out, the next day that spot will be crowded and they will have to fish somewhere else. You can't blame such a man for not revealing where he caught his fish. It's not that he wants to be selfish or greedy and keep the place to himself—he'll often tell a friend or two where he got the fish and extend an invitation to come along the next day—but he knows that if he tells a stranger and the word spreads around, in a short time there may be a hundred anglers trying to fish a spot where there is room for only three or four.

However, as a general rule, you will find that most surf anglers are pretty friendly and will gladly help a fellow angler. There's no sport like surf fishing for making friends. The pleasures gained in meeting new people and watching them grow into old friends through the years is really gratifying. If you walk along any beach and stop to talk to a surf angler, you'll get a hearty welcome. Most surf anglers enjoy swapping information and ideas with other surf anglers—quite a few will give you tips which will help you catch fish.

Surf fishing has a lot more to offer besides fish. True, we all like to go out and catch fish, but the very fact that it isn't easy to do this everytime, gives the sport a big appeal. Surf fishing is a challenge in many ways. First, the fisherman must study the weather, wind, tides, beaches, and shores so that his success will increase. (This may take a lifetime, and he will never really stop learning.)

Then again, the striped bass and some of the other surf fish are temperamental, unpredictable fish. A person can never be sure when they will show up or if they will cooperate by taking a lure or bait. Surf anglers have more blank days than most other salt-water fishermen, so they learn how to take the setbacks without getting discouraged. Surf anglers also work harder for their fish by walking beaches, climbing rocks, wading out, and making many casts. When they do get a fish they really appreciate it.

Another challenge offered by surf fishing is the danger present in the mighty ocean. When the angler climbs out on a rock jetty or wades out into water up to his hips, he is taking a risk: one big wave can come along and wash him out to sea. Also, he can slip on a rock and hurt himself. Surf fishing is more rugged than other types of salt-water fishing, but this very element of danger and hardship adds zest to the sport.

Finally, there's the ocean and sky and sand with their scenic beauties. One doesn't have to catch fish to really appreciate such things as a colorful sunrise or sunset, cloud formations over a blue sea, giant waves rolling in and smashing against a rocky shore, and graceful seagulls soaring and dipping with the wind. All these sights of nature are an added bonus which a surf angler enjoys.

After all, the main reason why people go fishing is to relax; to get away from cities, offices, factories, and homes; and enjoy a change of scenery as well as a day in the fresh air. Added to this is the benefit of exercise. If you do catch fish and have some fun then your day is really complete. Even should you return tired and—disappointingly—with no fish, remember that you were out in the open for hours where the body and mind enjoyed a change from the daily routine.

Index